Practical instructional design for open learning materials

A modular course covering – Open learning
                           – Computer-based training
                           – Multimedia

Nigel Harrison

McGRAW-HILL BOOK COMPANY

London · New York · St Louis · San Francisco · Auckland
Bogotá · Caracas · Lisbon · Madrid · Mexico · Milan
Montreal · New Delhi · Panama · Paris · San Juan · São Paulo
Singapore · Sydney · Tokyo · Toronto

Published by
McGRAW-HILL Book Company Europe
Shoppenhangers Road, Maidenhead, Berkshire, SL6 2QL, England
Telephone 01628 23432
Fax 01628 770224

British Library Cataloguing in Publication Data
Harrison, Nigel
    Practical Instructional Design for Open
    Learning Materials: Modular Course
    Covering – Open Learning, Computer-based
    Training, Multimedia. – 2Rev.ed. –
    (McGraw-Hill Training Series)
    I. Title   II. Series
    371.3078

    ISBN 0-07-709055-1

Library of Congress Cataloging-in-Publication Data
Harrison, Nigel
    Practical instructional design for open learning materials: a
modular course covering open learning, computer-based training,
multimedia / Nigel Harrison.
       p.   cm. – (McGraw-Hill training series)
    Includes bibliographical references and index.
    ISBN 0-07-709055-1
    1. Employees–Training of–Planning.   2. Instructional systems–
Design.   3. Computer-assisted instruction.   I. Title.   II. Title:
Open learning.   III. Series.
HF5549.5.T7H32   1995
658.3´12404–dc20   94-34853
                                                      CIP

12345 MPM 97654

Printed and bound in Great Britain at Multiplex Medway Ltd., Kent

PRACTICAL INSTRUCTIONAL DESIGN FOR OPEN LEARNING MATERIALS

Details of these and other titles in the series are available from:
The Product Manager, Professional Books, McGraw-Hill Book Company Europe,
Shoppenhangers Road, Maidenhead, Berkshire SL6 2QL
Tel: 0628 23432 Fax: 0628 770224

Contents

Series preface

Training and development are now firmly centre stage in most organizations, if not all. Nothing unusual in that—for some organizations. They have always seen training and development as part of the heart of their businesses—but more and more must see it that same way.

The demographic trends through the 1990s will inject into the marketplace severe competition for good people who will need good training. Young people without conventional qualifications, skilled workers in redundant crafts, people out of work, women wishing to return to work—all will require excellent training to fit them to meet the job demands of the 1990s and beyond.

But excellent training does not spring from what we have done well in the past. T&D specialists are in a new ball game. 'Maintenance' training— training to keep up skill levels to do what we have always done—will be less in demand. Rather, organization, work and market change training are now much more important and will remain so for some time. Changing organizations and people is no easy task, requiring special skills and expertise which, sadly, many T&D specialists do not possess.

To work as a 'change' specialist requires us to get to centre stage—to the heart of the company's business. This means we have to ask about future goals and strategies, and even be involved in their development, at least as far as T&D policies are concerned.

This demands excellent communication skills, political expertise, negotiating ability, diagnostic skills—indeed, all the skills a good internal consultant requires.

The implications for T&D specialists are considerable. It is not enough merely to be skilled in the basics of training, we must also begin to act like business people and to think in business terms and talk the language of business. We must be able to resource training not just from within but by using the vast array of external resources. We must be able to manage our activities as well as any other manager. We must share in the creation and communication of the company's vision. We must never let the goals of the company out of our sight.

In short, we may have to grow and change with the business. It will be hard. We shall have to demonstrate not only relevance but also value for money and achievement of results. We shall be our own boss, as accountable for results as any other line manager, and we shall have to deal with fewer internal resources.

The challenge is on, as many T&D specialists have demonstrated to me over the past few years. We need to be capable of meeting that challenge. This is why McGraw-Hill Book Company Europe have planned and launched this major new training series—to help us meet that challenge.

The series covers all aspects of T&D and provides the knowledge base from which we can develop plans to meet the challenge. They are practical books for the professional person. They are a starting point for planning our journey into the twenty-first century.

Use them well. Don't just read them. Highlight key ideas, thoughts, action pointers or whatever, and have a go at doing something with them. Through experimentation we evolve; through stagnation we die.

I know that all the authors in the McGraw-Hill Training Series would want me to wish you good luck. Have a great journey into the twenty-first century.

ROGER BENNETT
Series Editor

About the series editor

Roger Bennett has over 20 years' experience in training, management education, research and consulting. He has long been involved with trainer training and trainer effectiveness. He has carried out research into trainer effectiveness, and conducted workshops, seminars, and conferences on the subject around the world. He has written extensively on the subject including the book *Improving Trainer Effectiveness*, Gower. His work has taken him all over the world and has involved directors of companies as well as managers and trainers.

Dr Bennett has worked in engineering, several business schools (including the International Management Centre, where he launched the UK's first master's degree in T&D), and has been a board director of two companies. He is the editor of the *Journal of European Industrial Training* and was series editor of the ITD's *Get In There* workbook and video package for the managers of training departments. He now runs his own business called The Management Development Consultancy.

Author's preface

Why this book?   Since the publication of *How to Design Effective Text Based Open Learning* and *How to Design Effective Computer Based Training*, technology has moved on. We now have multimedia, but there still seems to be a great deal of ignorance about the fundamental instructional design needed to make learning materials effective.

This book will help you by providing a systematic approach to the design of effective learning materials, whatever media you use.

It is not theory. We design Open Learning, computer-based training (CBT) and multimedia for a living. This is the practical approach that we use. It works!

Why a second edition?   This new edition contains up-to-date experience and examples. It combines the two original titles and adds a section on design for multimedia.

Nigel Harrison
Chief Executive
ACT Consultants Ltd
Sheffield Science Park
Arundel Street
Sheffield S1 2NS
0742 780798

Introduction

*This book is divided into six modules
reflecting the six phases of the systematic approach to design*

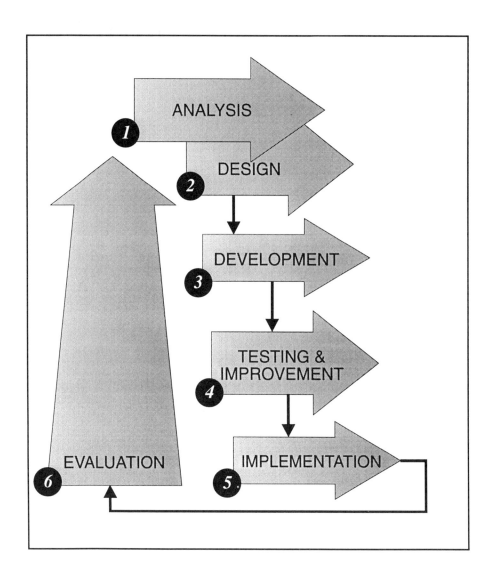

Who is it for?

New designers of Open Learning materials

Our target group is new training designers in organizations who want to use Open Learning to improve people's performance. This book is for you! We assume no background in instructional design.

Who else can use it?

Experienced designers

If you have some experience, take the self-assessment quiz to find the modules that are of relevance to you.

Computer-based training designers

The principles of good instructional design are the same for CBT as for any other medium. The only differences are the detailed screen design and flowcharting in Module 4.

Multimedia designers

We do not cover the features of the technology or authoring systems but this book includes the fundamentals of instructional design needed to make your multimedia solutions successful.

Trainers who design and run courses

The systematic approach to analysis and instructional design can be applied to any training method. It offers you a thorough approach to guarantee the quality and effectiveness of your training.

Training managers

The systematic approach can help you to analyse and design solutions to any performance problem. It will help you to be a better internal consultant, as well as providing a structure to manage your projects and allocate resources.

Are there any prerequisites?

Only the need to design learning materials. If you are not planning to design anything, it may be better to put the book down and pick it up again when you have a project in mind. It will mean more to you then.

You will need a project to work on for the practical exercises in Module 1.

What will it do?

'Walk through' all the stages involved in designing effective Open Learning materials.

What will you not be able to do?

Programme CBT, interactive video or multimedia. If you thought the book was about this, go back and get a refund.

Objective for the book

After working through the exercises using your own project,
when faced with an apparent training need you will be able to start
to design an effective Open Learning
solution which can include:

text-based Open Learning
CBT
books
workshops
multimedia
interactive video
workbooks
video
audio, etc.

What do I do next?

Do the self-assessment quiz on the next few pages to see how much you know already...

Self-assessment quiz

How to complete the self-assessment quiz

Rate how well you can answer each question

Give yourself a *2* if you can answer it fully, *1* if you think you know most of it, and *0* if you cannot answer it.

2	Yes	-	I can answer this fully
1	Partially	-	I think I know most of this
0	No	-	I can't answer this

Be honest!

This is for your needs only. No one else will see it.

Put down your first response.

It will give you a good idea of the modules you can use to develop skills.

There are five sets of questions, and a *score card* on page 12.

Self-assessment quiz

Can you...	Yes 2	Partially 1	No 0
a. Describe the difference between education and training?		☐	
b. List the main reasons why people have problems with performance?		☐	
c. Describe four essential elements of a measurable objective?		☐	
d. Describe the most appropriate writing style for Open Learning?		☐	
e. Describe what is involved in the testing and improvement phase?		☐	
f. Describe a simple method for ensuring that every module in your course follows the correct design process?		☐	
g. Explain when the key activities in summative evaluation take place?		☐	

Self-assessment quiz

Can you...	Yes 2	Partially 1	No 0

a. Name all the stages in a systematic approach to training design? ☐

b. Answer the question: 'Is training ever a solution on its own?' ☐

c. Describe the two different ways that objectives are used in Open Learning? ☐

d. Describe the key features of good page layout? ☐

e. Describe who should 'sign off' your draft materials before they are used for testing? ☐

f. Describe the training designer's involvement in implementation? ☐

g. Name those with whom you hold summative evaluations? ☐

Self-assessment quiz

Can you...	Yes 2	Partially 1	No 0
a. Name the focus that will ensure that training is effective?		☐	
b. Name the term used to describe the difference between what people are doing now and what you want them to be able to do?		☐	
c. Describe the two fundamental types of learning which affect your choice of method?		☐	
d. Describe the key features of good screen design?		☐	
e. Describe the format material should be in for small group testing?		☐	
f. State when you would find out about environmental factors which might hinder implementation?		☐	
g. Describe when you set up data collection for evaluation?		☐	

Self-assessment quiz

Can you...

	Yes 2	Partially 1	No 0

a. **Name five training methods that Open Learning can involve?** ☐

b. **Describe the difference between target group and target description?** ☐

c. **Name the method you always consider first when choosing medium?** ☐

d. **Produce a flowchart for a CBT lesson?** ☐

e. **State the technical name of the testing and improvement stage?** ☐

f. **Estimate how long an Open Learning project will take?** ☐

g. **Describe why trainers often find evaluation difficult?** ☐

Self-assessment quiz

	Yes 2	Partially 1	No 0

Can you...

a. Describe the difference between Open Learning and distance learning? ☐

b. Name the five criteria used to assess whether Open Learning may be an appropriate solution? ☐

c. Describe the essential elements in structuring a unit of learning? ☐

d. Describe the common page or screen types in any Open Learning solution? ☐

e. Estimate how long to allow for the testing and improvement stage? ☐

f. Describe all the roles to be included on a design project plan? ☐

g. Describe what you evaluate in evaluation? ☐

Let's see how you did...

How well did you do?

Score your rating

Add up your scores and look at page 13 to see how well you did.

Question	Page					Total
	7	8	9	10	11	
a.	☐	☐	☐	☐	☐	a. ☐
b.	☐	☐	☐	☐	☐	b. ☐
c.	☐	☐	☐	☐	☐	c. ☐
d.	☐	☐	☐	☐	☐	d. ☐
e.	☐	☐	☐	☐	☐	e. ☐
f.	☐	☐	☐	☐	☐	f. ☐
g.	☐	☐	☐	☐	☐	g. ☐

This book is divided into six learning modules, plus an introduction.

The questions in the quiz relate to the following modules.
Transfer your total scores to here.

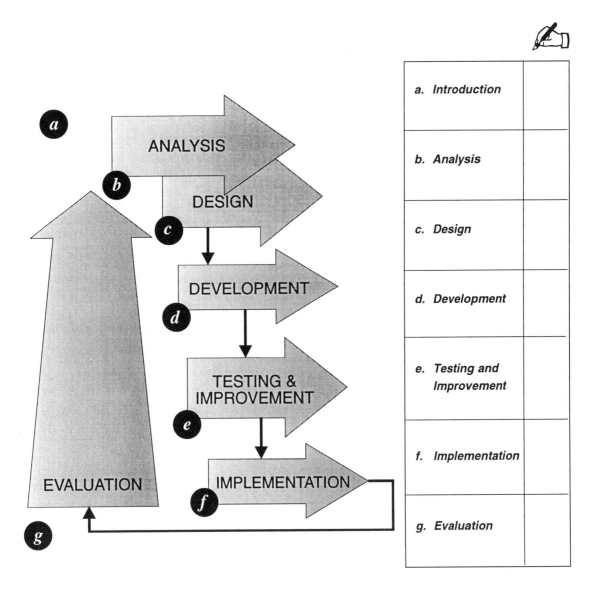

a. Introduction	
b. Analysis	
c. Design	
d. Development	
e. Testing and Improvement	
f. Implementation	
g. Evaluation	

What your score means

Score		
8 - 10	**Excellent**	You have an excellent grasp of the principles in this module and you do not need to look at it.
6 - 8	**Work needed**	Do this module and make sure you can pass the test.
0 - 6	**Start at the beginning**	Study this module thoroughly.

Use your scores to plan your learning.

If possible, discuss with your manager or a colleague how to incorporate on-the-job learning into your personal development.

Now let's check your understanding of the following terms:

- *Education*

- *Training*

- *Open Learning*

What is the difference between education and training?

Write a short definition of the following:

Education is:

Training is:

Open Learning is:

Answers

Education is:

Imparting core skills and knowledge to be built upon.

Training is:

Skills and knowledge to raise people's performance, often organized from the trainer's perspective.

Open Learning is:

Individualized instruction which is open to all; it is:
- *designed from the point of view of the learner rather than the trainer*
- *available in short, self-instructional modules which can be studied by individuals at their own pace, place and time*
- *structured to give the learner control over his or her learning*

Open Learning is a general term for an approach rather than for any specific medium or method.

What is the difference between education and training?

What would you think if your child said he or she had been having sex training at school today?
The difference between education and training is that training is about improving **performance** whereas education is about **knowledge.**

This difference is critical to the design of effective learning materials. Most senior managers hold the view that training is similar to education and that everyone is qualified to design training solutions. You just need to have an expert to present a subject to a group of others and tell them how to do it.

Notice that the main focus here is on knowledge and 'telling them', rather than improving performance and learning. The power and status belong to the trainer or educator, not the learner. The application of the knowledge is left to the student to sort out on his or her own.

This 'educational' view of training still exists and you can still attend 'training courses' given by subject matter experts where the trainee is essentially passive. How many managers have you heard say, 'Oh, we need some more training on X, get Sarah Smith, she knows all about it.' Little wonder that some trainers fall into the trap of the 'educational' style of training because this is what their superiors expect. To be fair to everyone involved, we can only see the world based on our own experience. Therefore, if you have only experienced formal education and classroom training, this is all you can see.

So what is training?

Training is about the **application of knowledge and skill to raise performance.** Sex training involves some practical improvement and the application of skill, not just knowledge.

It is not an end in itself; it only deals with 'how-to' improve people's performance.

The two essential elements of training are:

- *people*
- *performance*

In simple terms 'training' is about **helping people to do things better.**

What is learning?

Learning is what people do to develop their skills and knowledge in order to do things better.

So what is Open Learning?

Well, the power in education belongs to the teacher:

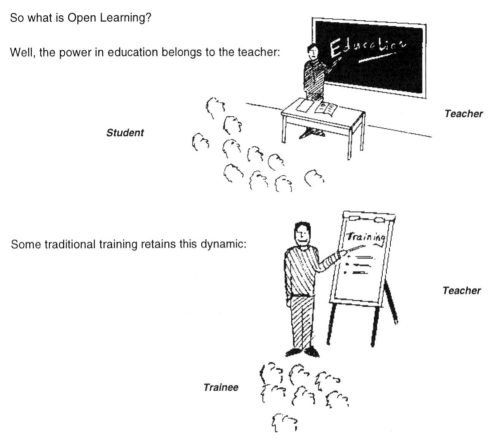

Teacher

Student

Some traditional training retains this dynamic:

Teacher

Trainee

However, in Open Learning the focus of power is shifted from the trainer to the learner (there is no trainer) and the trainer's role is to design effective learning materials that the learner can use to improve his or her performance.

Learning Materials

Designer

Learner

What is the difference between Open Learning and distance learning?

In pure terms Open Learning is *open* to all, like the Open University. Learners can choose what, how and when they learn.

'Distance learning' applies to the materials that allow people to learn away from a source of expertise or training. It will usually be on a single topic, have a clear performance improvement objective and, although it may give the learner options over time and place, it will be for a specific target group, *not* open to all.

In industry and commerce, it is more usual to have distance learning because of the *specified target groups;* however, the term is used very loosely. We use the term 'Open Learning' because this is the accepted way of talking about distance learning materials.

Open Learning is a very general term which can involve a variety of media:

*   books
*   CBT
*   multimedia
*   interactive video
*   workbooks
*   audio, etc.

We use the term loosely to mean any mix of media designed to be used by individual learners to improve their performance.

An outdated focus

Poor training and Open Learning is often due to a focus on the needs of the ***trainer*** rather than the ***learner***. Many Open Learning materials are nothing more than 'teaching' via another medium. To produce effective Open Learning we need to 'get inside the shoes' of the learner and design relevant, interactive and effective materials that he or she can use.

Trainers, leave your egos here!

You are now a learning materials designer. It is the learner who is important and your job is to help him or her to acquire the knowledge and skill needed to do things better.

The correct focus!

Remember that training only deals with 'how to' achieve something else. It is not important in its own right. What matters is **helping people to do things better**, i.e. perform better.

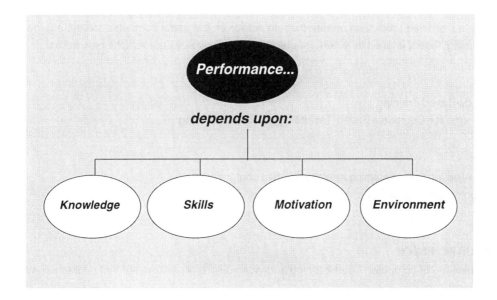

Training is only one method of helping people to acquire the knowledge and skills needed to raise performance.

It is not an end in itself

This is so important because many poor learning materials are written from the perspective of education and knowledge. The correct focus for effective materials is always to keep in mind the performance that you want to achieve and the people who are to achieve it.

Some training jargon explained

CD-ROM
Compact Disc Read Only Memory

Multimedia
CD-ROM has allowed more than one medium to deliver on the same computer screen, e.g. computer-aided learning, video, interactive video, graphics, text, high-quality photographs plus audio.

TBT
Technology-Based Training
Another name for Computer-Based Technology to deliver training.

CBT
Computer-Based Training, which actually has two components:
* Computer-Aided Learning
* Computer-Managed Learning

Interactive video
The combination of computer-aided learning and video disc which allows student interaction with a video through questions.

Virtual reality
A combination of hardware and software for creating or accessing a computer-created environment of sound and vision.

Books
The original distance learning method!

A systematic approach

Objective

> *By the end of this unit you will be able to label a diagram of the systematic approach and correctly match a set of definitions.*

For many trainers, the design of training may just be a matter of selecting the right person (subject matter expert) and scheduling a number of days to run a course. For traditional courses this may be enough, as skilled presenters can adapt their material as they go along. However, for any form of Open Learning, we need to be very systematic because the material has to be good enough to stand on its own.

A systematic approach can be applied to any training problem.

The systematic approach

This approach has six phases. Do you know any of them already?
DON'T PANIC. This question is NOT a test. It is just to get you thinking!
Label the following diagram as far as you can. The answers are on page 28.

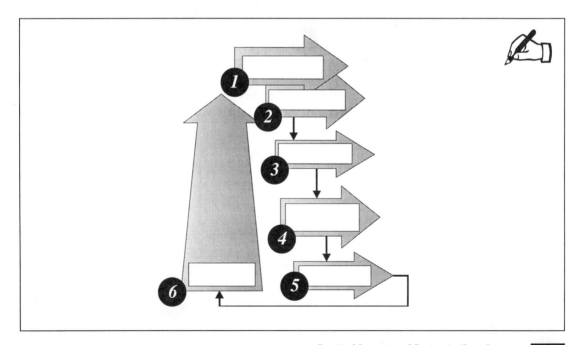

Answer

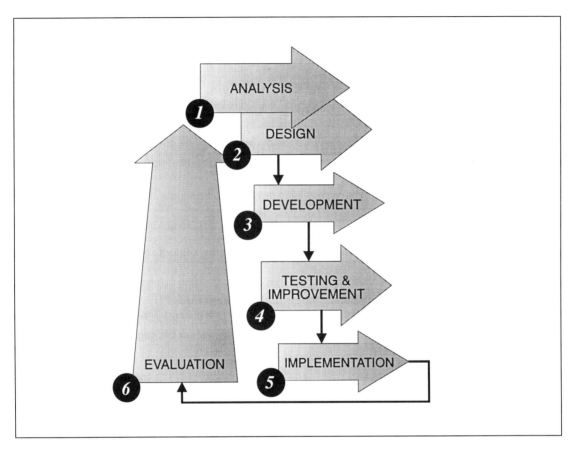

The phases in more detail

1. *Analysis*

We clarify what the performance problem is and select a number of solutions. Training is never a solution on its own. It always needs to be accompanied by some sort of management action and usually by information and reference material.

Once we have identified a training need, we can analyse the needs of the target group and define the final objective for the learning.

2. *Design*

We break down the topic into chunks (subordinate objectives) and then group these together into modules which can be taught together. Then we choose appropriate media and methods, and design appropriate tests and learning activities for each module.

3. *Development*

The draft material is produced, e.g. word processed, programmed, filmed or desktop published.

4. *Testing and improvement*

The draft material is tested with representatives from the target group and progressively improved.

5. *Implementation*

The material is used by the target audience in the real environment. Designers note what extra support is needed.

6. *Evaluation*

We check the success of the solutions in solving the original performance problem, i.e. can people do what the customer wanted them to be able to do?

Quiz

Can you match the phrase with the appropriate definition?

1. *Analysis* ☐

2. *Design* ☐

3. *Development* ☐

4. *Testing and improvement* ☐

5. *Implementation* ☐

6. *Summative evaluation* ☐

a. *The tested material is implemented with the target audience in the real environment.*

b. *We break down the topic into subordinate objectives and then group these into modules which can be taught together.*

c. *In this phase we clarify the performance problem and agree appropriate solutions.*

d. *The draft material is tested and improved.*

e. *The material is word processed, desktop published or programmed.*

f. *We check the success of the training in solving the original performance problem.*

Answers

Can you match the phrase with the appropriate definition?

1. **Analysis**   c

2. **Design**   b

3. **Development**   e

4. **Testing and improvement**   d

5. **Implementation**   a

6. **Summative evaluation**   f

a. **The tested material is implemented with the target audience in the real environment.**

b. **We break down the topic into subordinate objectives and then group these into modules which can be taught together.**

c. **In this phase we clarify the performance problem and agree appropriate solutions.**

d. **The draft material is tested and improved.**

e. **The material is word processed, desktop published or programmed.**

f. **We check the success of the training in solving the original performance problem.**

How did you do?

If you are having problems, refer back to page 29.
Complete this quiz correctly before you move on.

How to Design Effective Open Learning

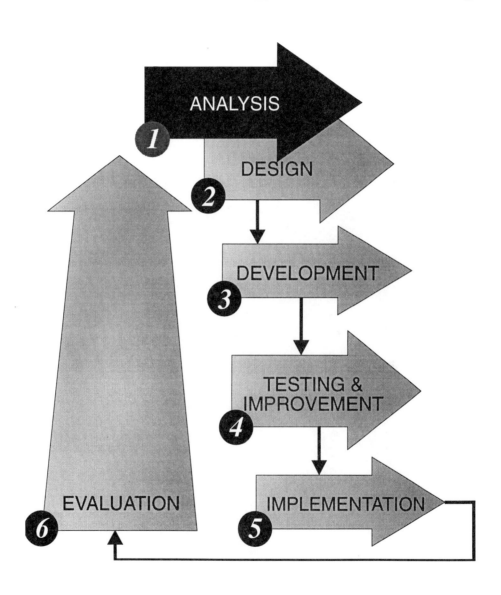

Module 1

Module 1 Analysis

- ***Unit 1***

  How to analyse a performance problem

- ***Unit 2***

  How to get inside the heads of your target group

- ***Unit 3***

  When is Open Learning appropriate?

- ***Unit 4***

  How to get your subject matter expertise

Unit 1

How to analyse a performance problem

Your customers will often come to you with a solution in mind. This is what we call **solutioneering.**

It is important, for your own self-protection and to ensure a successful solution, that you find the real problem and appropriate solutions without making assumptions.

The steps in this unit allow you to analyse the cause of any performance problem. Interested?

Objective

> *By the end of this unit you will have analysed all the possible causes for the performance problem in your project and have a list of necessary solutions.*

What is performance analysis?

Pioneered by Robert Mager and Peter Pipe, this is a series of steps to find the cause of any performance problem and all the solutions needed to solve it, not just training.

A project to work on?

This book cannot cover the skill of designing effective Open Learning. It can only give you a framework to work to and some aids to performance. However, if you use it to work on a real project and get someone to give you feedback and guidance, you can start to develop your skill.

Choose a topic where you know enough about the people's performance concerned.

It may be better to use a hobby, rather than a work-based topic, so that you can concentrate on the learning points rather than getting bogged down in the material.

Get some help!

The best way to learn is to get together with a colleague or tutor and work on the same topic. One of you needs to know enough about the subject matter to answer the other's questions.

Try to get someone to agree to support you in your learning, even if it is only someone with whom to discuss your answers. You can do it on your own but it is much better to get some help.

From now on you are going to work on your own project.

We have included an example of salespeople selling a mythical insurance product to doctors, called Doctors' Professional Insurance ('DPI').

Your project

If you haven't got a project, stop reading and go and get one!

What is the title of your project?
e.g. Doctors' Professional Insurance ('DPI')

1. Briefly describe the problem

    e.g.   *Information and marketing material is scarce and the salesforce is not selling enough of this sophisticated product*

2. Describe who is involved

    e.g.   *Experienced sales consultants and service representatives*

A system diagram

3. Sometimes it helps to draw a diagram of everyone involved in the problem, i.e. the system.

   Put a line around the main players involved in the performance that you want to do something about.

   Try drawing a system diagram for your project.

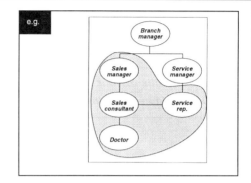

4. Describe what the main people are doing at the moment (the existing performance)

   e.g.   *Only a few sales consultants are selling this product at the moment*
          Service reps are not passing on any leads
          Branches are not hitting targets for sales. Company sells £½m this year

5. Describe what your customer wants them to be doing (the desired performance)

   e.g.   *All salespeople can sell this product*
          Company sales target of £3.5m achieved for DPI

6. How will your customer know when they can do this?

   e.g.   *All salespeople pass the test and are licensed to sell DPI*
          Annual sales targets achieved for all regions for DPI

What are the causes of the performance gap?

Reasons for low performance are usually a combination of the following, in this order:

- **Poor information/unclear expectations**
- **Difficult environment/inadequate equipment**
- **Poor incentives**
- **Lack of knowledge**
- **Lack of skills**
- **Poor motivation**

Note that 'performance gap' does not imply deficiencies in people. Most people want to do a good job.

What we can tackle with training is the lack of knowledge and skills. But how do we deal with the other causes of low performance?

First, let's quantify the problem a bit more...

7. **Now describe the effect of doing nothing**

    e.g.   *Sales will remain static, branches will not meet targets*

8. **Finally, estimate the cost of the gap if it remains**

    e.g.   *Lose potential sales of £3m*

              Company will fail to establish itself in an expanding market

9. **Is it worth doing something about?**

[Questions adapted from Mager and Pipe's *Analysing performance problems* - 1990]

What solutions could close this gap?

We could:

- **provide better information**
- **improve the environment, equipment, etc.**
- **provide better incentives**
- **reduce the task**
- **provide performance aids, e.g. checklists, diagrams, flowcharts, etc.**
- **provide practice, feedback and coaching**
- **encourage on-the-job training**
- **provide training**

Training is last on the list because it is expensive. Often simpler, more effective solutions can be found.

The danger of only implementing a training solution is that it may fail to achieve the desired performance because it fails to address other key causes for the performance gap!

Customers often have unrealistic expectations of training solutions (virtually setting them up to fail). If you are finding it difficult to meet all these expectations then it is probable that there was inadequate analysis of the causes of low performance in the first place.

On the next page is a superb performance aid. Use it to analyse the causes of the performance gap in your project. List all the possible solutions on page 46.

Performance analysis flowchart (based on Mager and Pipe's performance analysis flowchart, 1979)

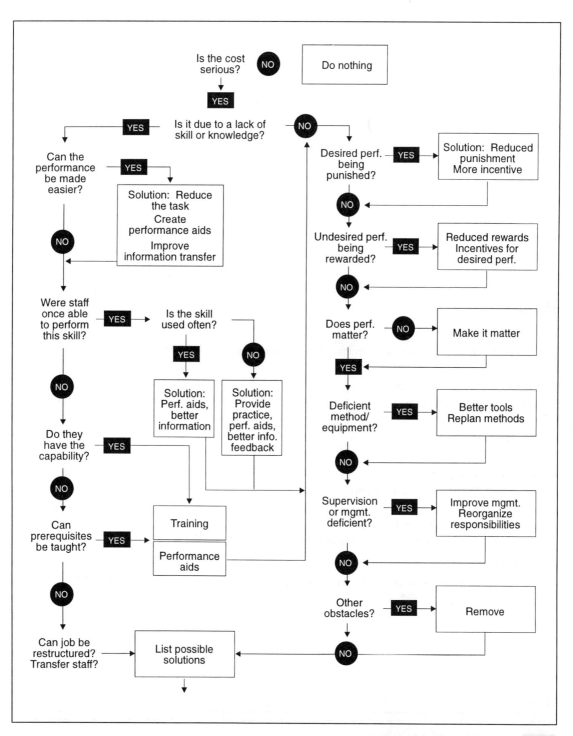

> **List all the solutions and estimate how much each will cost. Suspend judgement as to their feasibility.**
>
> *e.g.   Improve marketing brochures   20k*
> *Train all sales consultants in DPI   100k*
> *Introduce better rates of commission   self-funding*
> *Train service reps to spot opportunities   30k*

Reality

Get together with your partner, and eliminate the solutions that fail this reality filter:

*   Are any impossible to implement?
*   Is the cost greater than the benefit?

Highlight those which:

*   we can easily implement
*   will give us best results for minimum effort

> **Which solutions are you left with?**
> *e.g. Ask marketing to improve marketing brochures and introduce better rates of commission   20k*
>
> *While we:*
>
> *start to design a training programme to improve the performance of the sales teams, i.e. all sales consultants and service reps*

Action plan

What do we need to do next?

	Who	When
e.g. Contact marketing and find out what plans they have to improve the material. Start to design a training programme to improve the performance of sales teams		

If this is how to analyse a performance problem, what is a Training Needs Analysis?

Training Needs Analysis is an inaccurate term because *training* never has **needs**. Only **people** have needs. Training is a 'how to' achieve something else, not an end in itself.

However, you can safely assume that there is a need for training when it is a **new performance** and you know that the target group does not have the knowledge and skills to perform.

Even then it is dangerous to think in terms of a Training Needs Analysis because you might shut out alternative solutions other than the training group's needs. TNA is dangerous! **Always think performance analysis**. Not training!

So what do I do when I want some training?

When you have isolated parts of the problem that can be tackled by training, i.e. those that need knowledge and skill, you can safely write a final objective for the training element of the solution, e.g.:

All salespeople pass the licence test on the knowledge and skills required to sell DPI.

What about improving and maintaining existing performance?

We have covered how to solve specific performance problems and shown that training is appropriate for new performances, but what about maintaining existing performance?

In this case the target group probably has the knowledge and skills to do the job so the biggest impact on continuing performance is **motivation.**

The most important thing that drives continuous performance is ***self-concept.*** A salesperson who thinks of him or herself as a 'winner' will behave as a winner and exploit the opportunities in the environment almost despite any training. However, those with a poor self-concept may unconsciously set themselves up to fail and under-perform.

Can I handle this by training?

Not really!

If it is a complex motivational problem on an individual or organizational scale you are probably better off bringing in an occupational psychologist or organization development consultant. Training can only really tackle knowledge and skill comfortably. For complex culture and behaviour change, bring in the experts.

What you can do, however, is to design powerful visions into your materials and sell the benefits of achieving the objectives to the learner, so some motivation is built into the material.

The clearer, shorter, more relevant to the learner that you make the learning material, the better.

Write an aim or objective for the training part of your project

    e.g.   *By the end of the training, salespeople will be able to pass the licence test and prove that they can sell DPI in training scenarios*

Summary

How to analyse a performance problem

- Customers who ***solutioneer*** often ask:

    - Who is involved?
    - What are they doing now?
    - What do you want them to do?

- Reasons for the gap:

    - Poor information/unclear expectations
    - Difficult environment/inadequate equipment
    - Poor incentives
    - Lack of knowledge
    - Lack of skills
    - Poor motivation

- Use Mager and Pipe's performance analysis flowchart to list all solutions

- Put these through a reality filter

- Extract the knowledge and skill element that you can tackle with training

- Write an objective for the training element (if any)

Unit 2

How to get inside the heads of your target group

Objective

By the end of this unit you will be able to:

state the difference between target population and target group
describe the target group for your project
name three of the five questions that you might use to describe your target group

What is the difference between target population and target group?

The target population for your project is **all the people who may use it,** e.g. from sales manager to sales representative. However, you cannot design the course with the needs of a number of people in mind. So you need to 'target' the **main users of the solution,** say salespeople, and aim it at them. The target group is usually the **largest** group or the **most important in influencing the desired performance.**

The rest of your target population will be able to use the course but you will have stated that it was not designed for them.

If you do not define your target group clearly then you will run into problems with the design. Examples which may be ideal for supervisors will not suit managers or clerks. If you do not state who you designed the course for, then you leave yourself open to criticism.

You may be able to cope with different groups by producing different versions of the same course, so that people can see what is in the course without needing to work all the way through it.

Describe the target group of your project using the checklist on the following pages

Remember, these are only prompts. Ignore questions that do not work for you.

Think back to our system diagram

The most important person who is in contact with the customer and effects the end result (DPI sales) is the sales consultant.

Sales consultants form the target group.

Who is in the target population?
e.g. Sales managers, sales consultants, doctors, service reps, are all in the target population

Who is in the target group?
e.g. Sales consultants

The quality and the effectiveness of your learning package will depend on how well you can 'get into the head' of the learner.

For example, what you find out here will influence your screen designs. Will they be set in the workshop or on the battlefield? Would your target group appreciate cartoons or not?

It all depends on how well you understand what motivates your target group.

This is what we found out about our sales consultants.

Salespeople

Approx. 2500 throughout the UK
40 per cent annual wastage

Age 24-35, mainly male

Earn 12K basic, then commission

Very limited formal education, GCSE

Most people didn't choose the profession

Many have failed in other jobs

Have been asking for training and marketing material

Very busy in evenings. Have time in the office. Like quick, interactive games. All offices have learning rooms and multimedia kits. Learning must be able to be done in short bursts. Are interested in gaining qualifications for salespeople and like anything with direct applicability to improving their sales. If the top performers are seen doing training, everyone wants it.

Very status- and money-conscious.

Highly motivated to succeed but fear traditional education. All have laptop computers.

General

Job title

How old are they?

Sex

Education

Attitudes

Have people asked for training?

Have people had training before?

How did they react?

Do people prefer to set aside time for training all at once, or to find the time in small chunks?

Do people prefer to go away for training?

Do people associate training with formal, school-like methods?

What would encourage people to take part in training?

What other activities would compete with training time?

What are people's attitudes towards their work?

How do people change courses to make them more enjoyable for themselves?

What unrealistic preconceptions might they have about training?

What training or learning materials have worked well for this group in the past?

Education

What experience of formal education and training do people have?

What are their standards of literacy, numeracy?

Are they computer literate?

What motivates your target group?

What would people count as an achievement?

What do people mean by 'I am a success'?

Whose good opinions or respect do they value?

What things do people think affect their standing with their peers?

Interests

What do they do when not working?

What do they talk about?

What could hinder their learning?

General state of health?

Colour blindness?

Can people concentrate? For how long?

Are people easily distracted?

Where are they?

Do they work from home?

Do they spend a lot of time travelling?

Quiz

1. **What is the difference between a target population and a target group?**

   A target population is:

   A target group is:

2. **Have you described the target group for your project?**

   ✓

   No

   Yes

3. **From memory, name at least five questions that you might use to get inside the heads of a target group**

   1.

   2.

   3.

   4.

   5.

Answers

1. **What is the difference between a target population and a target group?**

   A target population is:

   > *All the people who may use it*

   A target group is:

   > *The main users for the solution; usually the largest*
   > *or most important group*

2. **Have you described the target group for your project?**

No	**Do it! If you cannot answer the questions, go and ask someone who knows the target group**
Yes	**Move on to Unit 3**

3. **From memory, name at least five questions that you might use to get inside the heads of a target group**

   1.   *Check with pages 58 and 59*

   2.

   3.

   4.

   5.

Unit 3

When is Open Learning appropriate?

Objective

> *By the end of this unit, given a need to assess the feasibility of an Open Learning project, you will be able to find a checklist of key factors which indicate that Open Learning may be an effective solution*

When is Open Learning appropriate?

Use this checklist to see if Open Learning is appropriate for your project

	e.g. financial salespeople ✓/✗	*your project* 🖊
Have you got a large target group? So that you can justify the large one-off investment	✓	☐
Are they geographically dispersed? Who would find training courses difficult to get to?	✓	☐
Is the training to be repeated often? Either for new starters or refresher training	✗	☐
Has the material a decent shelf-life? So there will not be many updates	✓	☐
Will people enter training with variable levels of skill and knowledge?	✗	☐

If you have a majority of ticks, Open Learning may help.

However, do your learners have the required:

• **literacy?**	✓	☐
• **study skills?**	?	☐
• **self-discipline?**	?	☐
• **confidence?**	?	☐
• **motivation?**	✓	☐

Could your learners benefit significantly from these features?

	e.g. financial salespeople ✓/✗	your project
They can learn at their own pace, place and time	✓	☐
Do they need to break study, e.g. to attend interviews, to start a new job?	✓	☐
It doesn't have the negative associations that traditional classroom teaching might have	✓	☐
It can help link training to work because you can do it at work and use real projects and exercises to work from	✓	☐

Is Open Learning appropriate for your project?

Why?

e.g.   It is probably the only thing that will work for this highly motivated but dispersed group of salespeople who have spare time during the day because most current sales are in the evening

What support do I need to plan for?

Support for learners from colleagues, line managers and tutors is vital. You plan for this in your design by identifying such people in your system diagram and target audience. You will probably have to produce some training for them on how to offer their support. But don't worry about this now, wait until the materials are being tested to assess what you will need.

If you want to set up a more formal Open Learning scheme, the following might help:

Open Learning in Industry (Flexible Learning Ltd, 1987) includes:

* how Open Learning can help you
* a strategy for introducing Open Learning
* selecting, adapting and developing an Open Learning package
* support for Open Learning
* managed Open Learning

How to Develop and Manage an Open Learning Scheme, Lewis, R. (CET, 1985)

Unit 4

How to get your subject matter expertise

Objective

By the end of this unit you will be able to identify:

a high performer

a subject matter expert (SME)

a signatory for your project

Existing material

Now you know who your target group is and roughly what it needs to be able to do (the desired performance), you have enough information to find out whether any of the material you need already exists. This need not necessarily BE material that you can use directly, but anything that covers part of the subject or gives you ideas for approaches to use.

> ***Note below any existing material that could be used for all or part of your project***
> *e.g. Existing marketing material on DPI*

You will need access to local expertise to help you design your solutions.

No one person will have all the required knowledge and skills for the complete training package. Identify your experts and involve them now.

Someone who can do the job well already, your high performer
e.g.   *Colin Trowson, Sales Consultant of the Year*

> **Name**

An expert in the subject, your subject matter expert (SME)
e.g.   *Fred Flint, Technical Officer, Medical Insurance*

> **Name**

A representative sample of the target group
e.g.   *Sheffield branch sales team*

>

Signatories: individuals who sign off the project stages, the customer who has to approve the final product
e.g.   *Nigel Ballard, Marketing Director (customer), Norma Jean, Compliance*

> **Names**

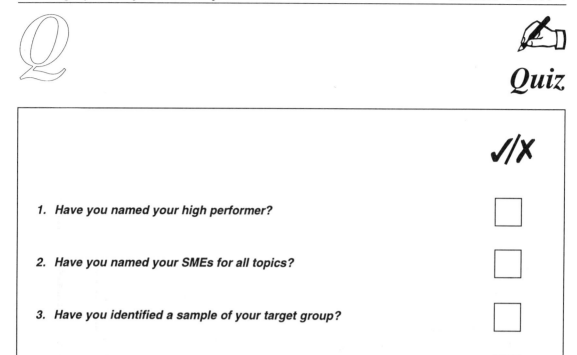

Quiz

	✓/✗
1. Have you named your high performer?	☐
2. Have you named your SMEs for all topics?	☐
3. Have you identified a sample of your target group?	☐
4. Have you defined who your customer is?	☐

The standard for this unit is to have done all of the above.

Summary

ACT ANALYSIS CHECKLIST

Have you:

Defined the problem as you see it.. ☐
Drawn a system diagram.. ☐
Identified the target group... ☐
Described the existing performance... ☐
Described the desired performance.. ☐
Estimated the value of the performance gap £.. ☐
Described the effect of doing nothing.. ☐
Investigated existing material... ☐
Listed all the possible solutions .... ☐
Identified own recommended solutions.. ☐

Identified   High performers... ☐
             Subject matter experts... ☐
             Target group sample.. ☐
             Sign off.. ☐

Listed the action needed

Action	Who	When

How to Design
Effective Open Learning

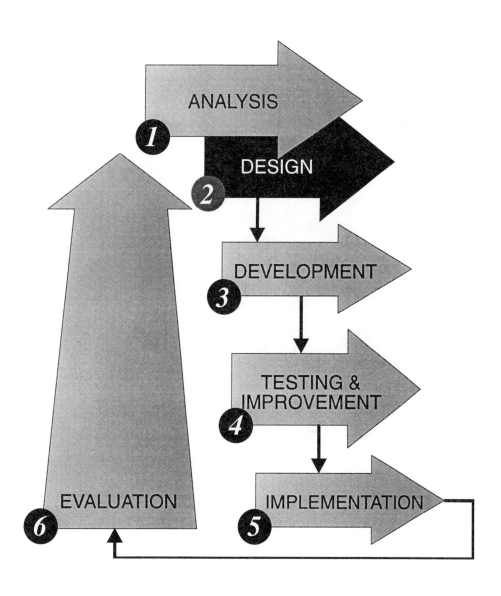

M o d u l e   2

Module 2 Design

- *Unit 1*

  How to write measurable objectives

- *Unit 2*

  Pyramid analysis

- *Unit 3*

  Selecting appropriate media

- *Unit 4*

  Starting the detailed design

- *Unit 5*

  Test question design

Unit 1

How to write measurable objectives

Objective

By the end of this unit you will be able to:

*describe the two ways that objectives are used
in designing Open Learning*

*state the four elements of a measurable
performance*

*state the phrase used to check whether an
objective is measurable*

write a measurable objective for your project

Objectives are used in two ways in Open Learning

1. Design objectives

This is designers' shorthand for all the elements that need to go into a successful design. They may be written in a long-winded technical way.

2. Learner's objectives

This is a motivating statement of what the learner will be able to do at the end of any unit of training. It is written in a friendly and inspiring way to help the learner to visualize him or herself carrying out the performance.

Measurable learning objectives are the key to effective training

Many so-called objectives are aims. For example:

'The objective of the seminar is that the students will gain an understanding of the manufacturing process.'

This is not an objective **because it is not measurable.**

There are four elements to a good objective:

Conditions

e.g. by the side of the road

Performance

e.g. change a wheel

Standards

e.g. within 15 minutes

Method of assessment

e.g. timed by passenger's watch

This method of splitting objectives into elements was pioneered by Robert Mager
(see *Preparing Instructional Objectives,* Mager, 1962), although he uses 'Criterion' to describe standards and method of assessment.

Objectives checklist

Conditions

| |
| |

✓/✗

**Are they
realistic?** ☐

Performance

| |
| |

**Can you ask
'Watch me'?** ☐

Standards

| |
| |

**Are they
measurable?** ☐

**Are they
appropriate?** ☐

Method of assessment

| |
| |

Specified? ☐

The elements in more detail

Conditions - A performance always happens under certain conditions

The nearer these conditions are to the actual situation, the better they will be. For example, it is one thing to be able to change a wheel in a warm, well-lit garage, but quite another to do the same task in the middle of the night by the side of the road. On the other hand, a trainee engineer will not be able to learn to repair a piece of equipment on the site unless he or she can first learn to repair it in the workshop. So conditions are used either to limit, or to enlarge, what a learner has to do: they must be *realistic.*

Performance - what the learner will be able to do

The performance must be observable. Words such as 'understand', 'appreciate', 'know' are useless. We cannot see anyone 'appreciating'. So use verbs of action. If you have any doubts, place 'watch me' before the verb describing the performance.

'Watch me ... understand this software.' **X**
'Watch me ... use Lotus 123 to produce a cash flow.' ✓

Make sure that the verb in your objective is the *desired performance* you had in mind.

Standards - how well must this performance be done?

* Standards must be *measurable* and *attainable*
* Set them too low and they will not be effective; too high and they will be demotivating, so start with a first stab and get them right by testing
* Standards must be appropriate for the topic, e.g. safety standards may be a 100 per cent standard. If an accident occurs, you do not get a second chance to do the task more carefully
* Always consider the level of performance needed in real life.

Method of assessment - what method will you use to assess?

Robert Mager stresses that we must specify the method of assessment as part of the standard, e.g.: Is it by the supervisor using a checklist or by a computer-based quiz? It makes a difference.

Example objective

Use the checklist to analyse the following objective:

> *Use PC payroll with training data to print a payroll summary so that your supervisor signs that it matches the example given exactly.*

1 Look for the conditions

'PC payroll with training data.'

2 Look for the performance

'Use PC payroll to print a payroll summary' describes what someone has to do.

3 Check for the standards

'Matches the example given exactly.'

4 Has the method of assessment been specified?

'Supervisor signs.'

This example contains the four elements of a good objective.

You should now be able to check any statement that claims to be an objective to see whether it contains these vital elements.

Objectives checklist

✓/✗

Conditions

Use PC payroll with training data

Are they realistic? ✓

Performance

Print a payroll summary

Can you ask 'Watch me?' ✓

Standards

Matches the example given exactly

Are they measurable? ✓

Are they appropriate? ✓

Method of assessment

Supervisor signs

Specified? ✓

Objectives for practice

Given the following four objectives, analyse each one using a blank checklist for each.

Check your answers after each attempt using the 'Check Yourself' sheets.

Your analysis should match ours (this is the only standard for this exercise, as you are still learning). If you have any difficulty, talk it over with a colleague.

---

1. **Given the example data entry forms, set up the stock, supplier and customer files and obtain a printout, so that the printout matches the entry form exactly.**

2. **By the time you complete this workbook you will be able to develop your skills in all areas of customer service.**

3. **From the user manual, identify correctly all five of the following components:**

    (a) mother board
    (b) fan
    (c) power supply
    (d) daughter boards
    (e) disk drives

4. **With a set of tools, and the reference manual, adjust the display to the correct focus, so that a set of 'Hs' appears sharp to your instructor.**

Given the example data entry forms, set up the stock, supplier and customer files and obtain a printout, so that the printout matches the entry form exactly.

Practice 1

Conditions

✓/X

Are they realistic? ☐

Performance

Can you ask 'Watch me'? ☐

Standards

Are they measurable? ☐

Are they appropriate? ☐

Method of assessment

Specified? ☐

Given the example data entry forms, set up the stock, supplier and customer files and obtain a printout, so that the printout matches the entry form exactly.

Answers

Conditions

> Given the example data and the entry forms

Are they realistic? ✓

Performance

> Set up the stock, supplier and customer files and obtain a printout

Can you ask 'Watch me'? ✓

Standards

> So that the printout matches the entry form exactly

Are they measurable? ✓

Are they appropriate? ✓

Method of assessment

Specified? ✗

2 By the time you complete this workbook you will be able to develop your skills in all areas of customer service.

Practice 2

✓/✗

Conditions

Are they realistic? ☐

Performance

Can you ask 'Watch me'? ☐

Standards

Are they measurable? ☐

Are they appropriate? ☐

Method of assessment

Specified? ☐

2

> By the time you complete this workbook you will be able to develop your skills in all areas of customer service.

Answers

✓/✗

Conditions

> By the time you complete this workbook

Are they realistic? **?**

Performance

> You will be able to develop your skills in all areas of customer service

Can you ask 'Watch me'? **✗**

Standards

Are they measurable? **✗**

Are they appropriate? **✗**

Method of assessment

Specified? **✗**

> **3** From the user manual, identify correctly all five of the
> following components:
> *(a) mother board (b) fan (c) power supply*
> *(d) daughter boards (e) disk drives*

Practice 3

✓/✗

Conditions

Are they
realistic? ☐

Performance

Can you ask
'Watch me'? ☐

Standards

Are they
measurable? ☐

Are they
appropriate? ☐

Method of assessment

Specified? ☐

3 From the user manual, identify correctly all five of the following components:
(a) mother board (b) fan (c) power supply
(d) daughter boards (e) disk drives

Answers

Conditions

From the user manual

✓/✗

Are they realistic? ✓

Performance

Identify all five of the following components:
(a) mother board (b) fan (c) power supply
(d) daughter boards (e) disk drives

Can you ask 'Watch me'? ✓

Standards

All five, correctly

Are they measurable? ✓

Are they appropriate? ?

Method of assessment

Specified? ✗

With a set of tools, and the reference manual, adjust the display to the correct focus, so that a set of 'Hs' appears sharp to your supervisor.

Practice 4

✓/✗

Conditions

Are they realistic? ☐

Performance

Can you ask 'Watch me'? ☐

Standards

Are they measurable? ☐

Are they appropriate? ☐

Method of assessment

Specified? ☐

With a set of tools, and the reference manual, adjust the display to the correct focus, so that a set of 'Hs' appears sharp to your supervisor.

Answers

✓/✗

Conditions

Given a set of tools, and the reference manual

Are they realistic? ✓

Performance

Adjust the display

Can you ask 'Watch me'? ✓

Standards

To the correct focus

Are they measurable? ✓

Are they appropriate? ✓

Method of assessment

So that a set of 'Hs' appears sharp to your supervisor

Specified? ✓

Quiz

1. **Describe the two ways that objectives are used in Open Learning.**

2. **What are the four elements of good objectives?**

1.
2.
3.
4.

3. **What phrase is used in front of the verb to check whether a performance is observable?**

4. **Analyse this objective:**
    On completion of this unit you will have a good knowledge of safety regulations when working underground.

Answers

1. **Describe the two ways that objectives are used in Open Learning.**

Design objectives	-	Shorthand design for the designer
Learner's objectives	-	Friendly description of what the learner will be able to do

2. **What are the four elements of good objectives?**

   1. Conditions

   2. Performance

   3. Standards

   4. Method of assessment

3. **What phrase is used in front of the verb to check whether a performance is observable?**

   'Watch me'

4. **Analyse this objective:**
   On completion of this unit you will have a good knowledge of safety regulations when working underground.

   Conditions
   On completion of this unit. **The conditions are precise**

   Performance
   You will have a good knowledge of safety regulations when working underground.
   But they are meaningless because the performance is not observable.

   Standards   **A better objective might be:**
   No standards have been set.   *On completion of this unit you will be able to answer accurately and*
                                      without hesitation 10 questions on the underground safety
   Method of assessment   *regulations to your safety office.*
   None

Now write a performance objective.

This comes straight from the desired performance.

e.g.   *A performance objective for financial consultants*

Example

Conditions

Given eight interviews with doctors over six months, accompanied by your sales manager

Are they realistic?

Performance

- *complete the DPI fact-find*
- *outline the benefits of DPI*
- *overcome common obstacles*
- *close the sale*

Can you ask 'Watch me'?

Standards

No technical errors in the fact-find
so that you make the sale in 80 per cent of cases with an identified need

Are they measurable?

Are they appropriate?

Method of assessment

Fact-find checked by technical officer

Sales manager evaluates closing rate for each accompanied sale. Achievement of standard will lead to licence to sell DPI

Specified?

Now write a performance objective for your project

Write the performance objective for your project.

What is the difference between a performance objective and a training objective?

Very little. You will see from our example that ***the main changes are the conditions.*** We cannot use real interviews so we use role-plays.

The rule is to ***keep as close to the real conditions*** as possible, e.g.:

Given eight multimedia role-play
simulations of interviews with doctors:

> ***Sales people will complete the DPI fact-find, outline the benefits of DPI, overcome common obstacles, close the sales***
>
> ***so that you make the sale in 80 per cent of cases with an identified need***
>
> ***and the computer rates your performance as satisfactory using a checklist***
>
> ***Achievement of the standard will lead to a provisional licence to sell DPI in accompanied sales***

On the next page, write a final training objective for your own project.

* Make sure it conforms to the standards set out in the checklist
* Show your objectives to a colleague

In the next unit we will see how to break down the topic into the subordinate or enabling objectives needed to achieve this final objective.

The training objective for my project

Conditions

□ ✓/✗

Are they
realistic? □

Performance

Can you ask
'Watch me'? □

Standards

Are they
measurable? □

Are they
appropriate? □

Method of assessment

Specified? □

Unit 2

Pyramid analysis

The objective you have written is the final objective for your project. The next step is to split up the topic into manageable chunks using a technique called **pyramid analysis.**

Objective

By the end of this unit, given your project's final objective, you will be able to draw a pyramid of objectives

(All the prerequisite knowledge and skills should be marked on the pyramid.)

Pyramid analysis is an invaluable technique that allows you to **split up a topic up into digestible chunks.** These chunks can then be combined into modules. You can then decide the order in which to teach them, and which medium to use.

It is a skill which needs practice.

Pyramids also help you to make sure that everything you should have is included in your design. The best way to do this is to **start with your final objective and work downwards.** Then you can be sure that everything you identify is essential to reaching that final objective and not just something you think it would be good for the learner to know. What you are actually doing is dividing a final objective into its subordinate or enabling objectives.

How to draw a pyramid

Take the final objective for your project and write this on the top of a large piece of paper.

Then ask the question:

'What does a person need to be able to do in order to do this?'

The answers go on the next level of your pyramid.

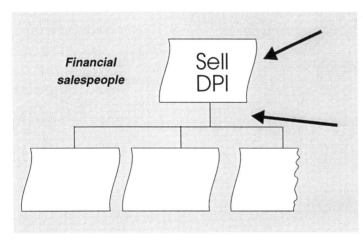

A short version of your final objective

Ask the question 'What does the target group need to be able to do in order to do this?'

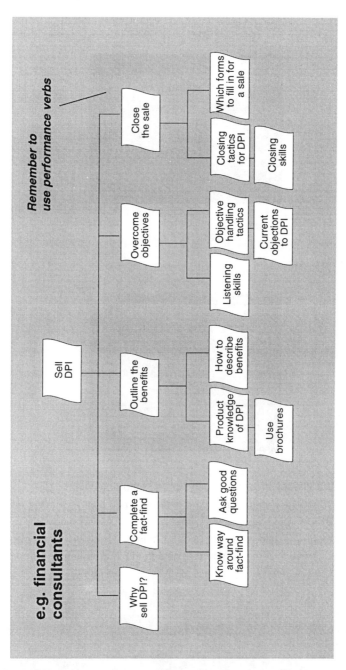

Helpful hints

1. Draw your pyramid with the guidance of a high performer
2. Use a large piece of paper and set aside at least one hour
3. Use small Post-it notes, so that you can move topics around. (You never get it right first time.)

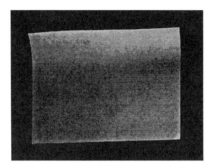

4. Write your objectives in shorthand form to try to keep the *real* words used by the high performer, e.g.:

5. Don't worry too much if it doesn't make much sense at the beginning.
   As long as you have the information on Post-it notes you can always move it around later.

6. Once you have a rough pyramid, take it to another high performer and your subject matter expert (SME) and improve it. You will find that having the information on Post-it notes helps.

Prerequisite knowledge and skills

Now that you have a pyramid of all the knowledge and skills needed to achieve the objective, you may be able to specify some topics as prerequisites for your course. For example, we don't want to cover listening skills or generic closing skills so we indicate these as prerequisites by a dotted line on our pyramid.

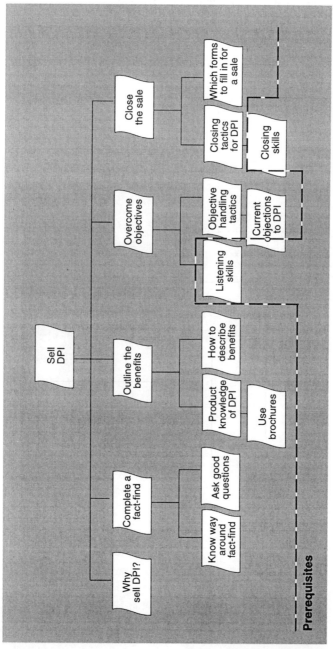

Group topics into modules

Now you have a pyramid. You can arrange topics together into groups that you can tackle at the same time.

There is no science to this. Just put things together that seem to involve similar performances. Use a pen to draw circles around common topics.

- Big groups will be modules
- Sub-groups will be units

Structure

We use the following:

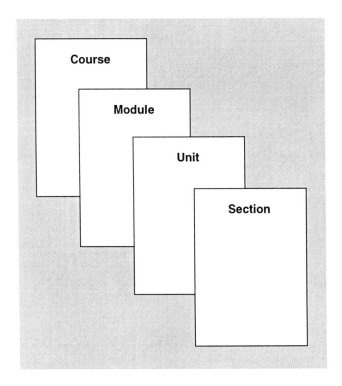

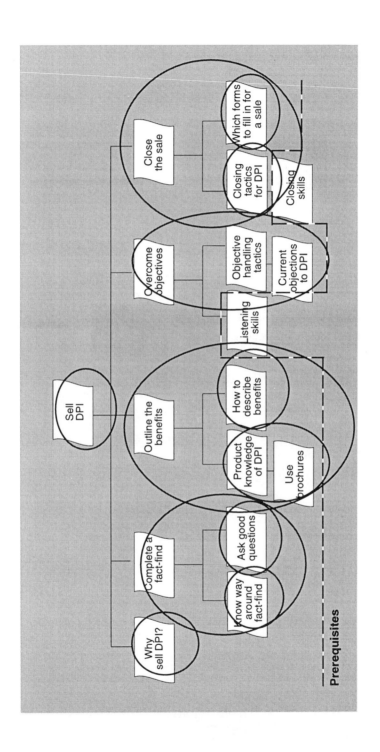

Order of learning

Annotate your diagram with module and unit numbers:

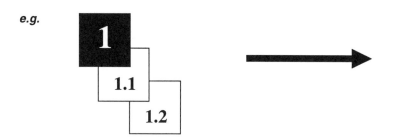

Don't forget that the final objective may be a module itself, usually the final exercise or test for the course.

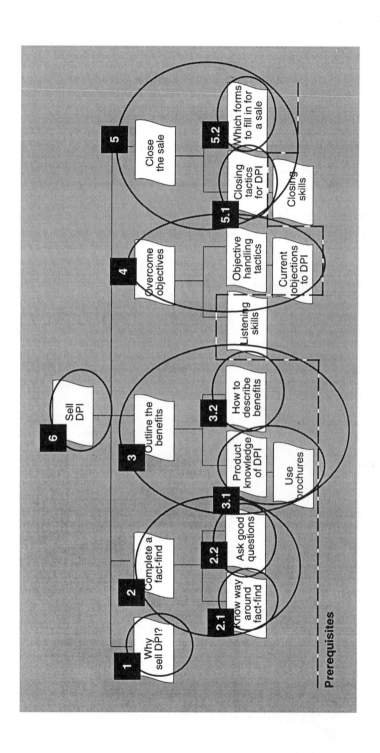

A learning map

So far, pyramids have been used for our purposes as designers (and they can get pretty messy). Now that you have an order of modules, you can represent them for the learner.

Re-draw your modules on a learning map, see page 113.

By convention, we start at the bottom and build up. Notice how the modules retain their active performance titles, like 'How to ...'. This keeps the topic alive. Notice also how modules can be of different sizes to represent importance or amount of content.

N.B.   Short-term memory will hold about nine items. This means that we can hold a pattern of nine things in our heads. So make your course nine or fewer modules in length and represent them in a diagram.

There are two examples of real pyramids on pages 114 and 115.

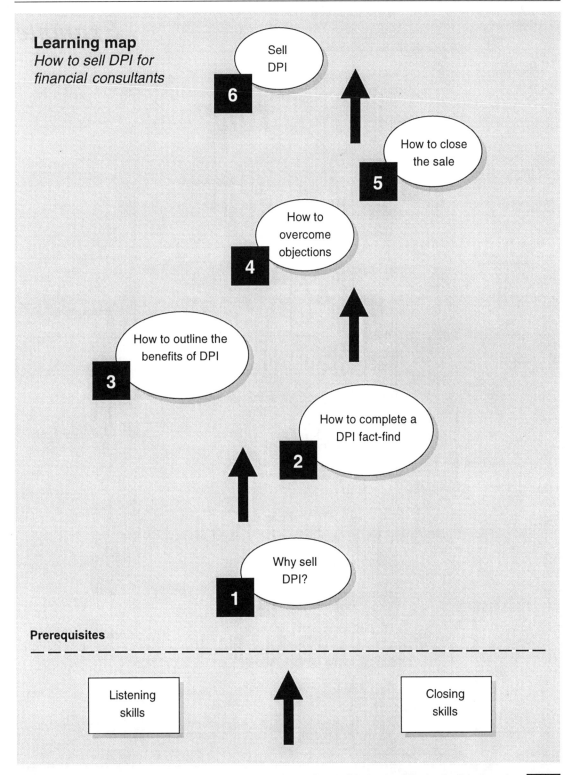

Learning map
*How to sell DPI for
financial consultants*

Sell
DPI

6

How to close
the sale

5

How to
overcome
objections

4

How to outline the
benefits of DPI

3

How to complete a
DPI fact-find

2

Why sell
DPI?

1

Prerequisites

Listening
skills

Closing
skills

Example

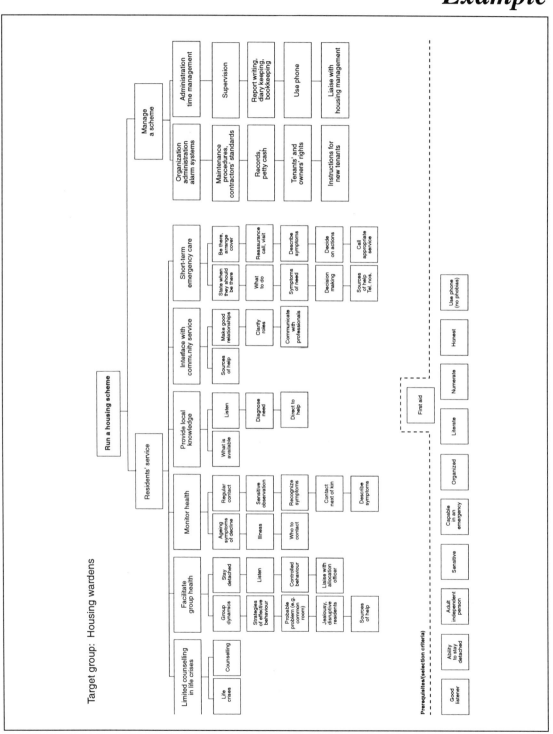

Target group: Housing wardens

Run a housing scheme

Residents' service

Facilitate group health
- Group dynamics
- Strategies of effective behaviour
- Probable problem (e.g. common room)
- Jealousy, disruptive residents
- Sources of help
- Stay detached
- Listen
- Controlled behaviour
- Liaise with allocation officer

Limited counselling in life crises
- Life crises
- Counselling

Monitor health
- Ageing symptoms of decline
- Illness
- Who to contact
- Contact next of kin
- Describe symptoms
- Regular contact
- Sensitive observation
- Recognize symptoms

Provide local knowledge
- What is available
- Diagnose need
- Direct to help
- Listen

Interface with community service
- Sources of help
- Clarify roles
- Communicate with professionals
- Make good relationships

Short-term emergency care
- State when they should be there
- What to do
- Symptoms of need
- Decision making
- Sources of help Tel. nos.
- Be there, arrange cover
- Reassurance call, visit
- Describe symptoms
- Decide on actions
- Call appropriate service

Manage a scheme
- Organization administration alarm systems
- Maintenance procedures, contractors' standards
- Records, petty cash
- Tenants' and owners' rights
- Instructions for new tenants
- Administration time management
- Supervision
- Report writing, diary keeping, bookkeeping
- Use phone
- Liaise with housing management

First aid

Prerequisites/(selection criteria)
- Good listener
- Ability to stay detached
- Adult independent person
- Sensitive
- Capable in an emergency
- Organized
- Literate
- Numerate
- Honest
- Use phone (no phobias)

Example

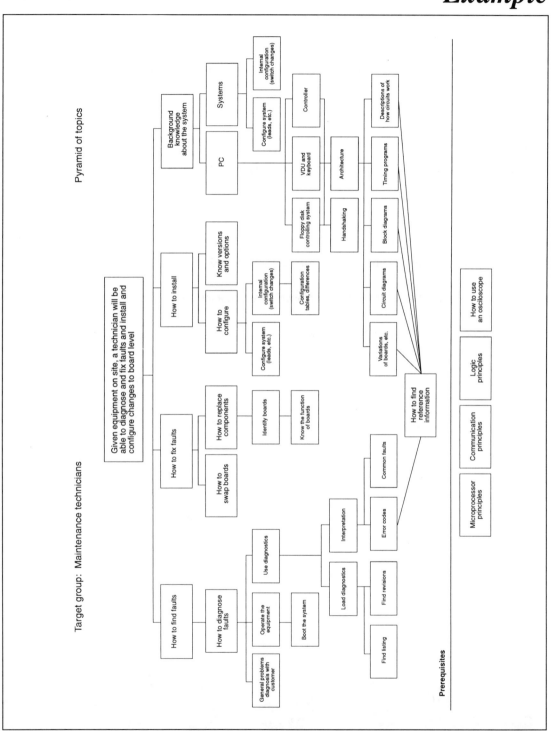

Pyramid of topics

Target group: Maintenance technicians

Given equipment on site, a technician will be able to diagnose and fix faults and install and configure changes to board level

Prerequisites

Summary

Drawing pyramids using a large piece of paper and Post-it notes is a very creative way of getting your high performers involved in the project. As you work together on the pyramid design you can 'see' the structure of the training emerge in front of your eyes. It can be very rewarding. Try it with your subject matter expert as well.

Now, on the blank sheet of paper, create a pyramid of topics for your project and include prerequisites

Remember:

*   What does a person need to be able to do in order to do this?

*   Use one small Post-it note for each topic. (It will save you a lot of rubbing out.)

That is the end of this unit of pyramid analysis.

Unit 3

Selecting appropriate media

Ever been confused about learning types, cognitive versus psychomotor, how to cope with learning styles? What is the best training method to use? Is multimedia better than classroom training? This unit answers these questions.

Objective

> *By the end of this unit you will be able to:*
>
> *demonstrate the two fundamentally different types of learning*
>
> *list the advantages and disadvantages of different types of media*
>
> *state what media-effective instruction always involves*
>
> *name the method that you always consider first*
>
> *make a list of performance aids used in everyday life*
>
> *state three of the four reasons for using performance aids*

The two fundamental types of learning are:

You need to know this because the way people learn skills is different from the way they acquire knowledge and this will affect your choice of medium on your learning map.

The difference is that skill can only be learned by **practice** and **feedback**, e.g. you might acquire the basic knowledge about how to kick a football, but you can only develop skill by trying it and getting feedback.

Knowledge can be acquired at a distance using books, etc., but skill needs practice.

Check for the potential to use performance aids

The next essential step in the design process is to consider the potential for using performance aids, like the performance analysis flowchart.

A performance aid can often reduce the training needed and so is very cost-effective. You use them:

1. ***To jog memory***
    e.g.   checklists, labels
             diagrams, codes
             mnemonics

3. ***To reduce complexity***
    e.g.   calculators, tables
             algorithms, procedures
             graphs, decision trees
             simulations, printed formats

2. ***To improve information***
    e.g.   different kinds of signals
             automatic reminders, rules
             blocking information that is
             not essential, feedback

4. ***To identify something quickly***
    e.g.   colours, labels, shapes

Save money with performance aids

Using performance aids can reduce or remove the need for training altogether.

In one case a company replaced a lesson on how to start up and shut down machinery with a table of colour-coded instructions which were stuck on each machine!

In another case of a new version of software, additional help screens and on-screen prompts removed the need for training altogether.

Exercise

We use performance aids all the time in everyday life.

List as many as you can think of, then compare them with our list on the next page.

Performance aids in everyday life:

Some examples of performance aids:

- the line on a beer glass

- the instructions around the outside of a digital watch

- road signs

- procedures

- quick reference cards

- templates on computer keyboards explaining function keys

- tables on the inside of washing machine lids explaining the different programmes

- visual displays on photocopiers which tell you what to do

- numbered parts inside a photocopier

- icons on a computer screen

- pilot's checklists

- shaped plugs which will only fit into the correct socket

- coloured casing for electrical wiring

- the London Underground map

- forms

- algorithms (like Mager and Pipe's performance analysis flowchart)

- the colour purple added to methylated spirits

Examples

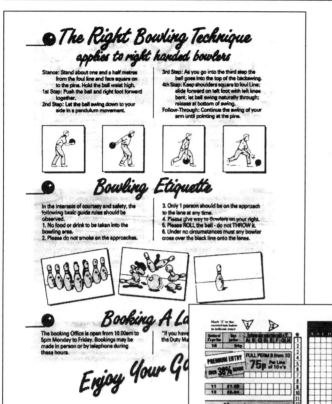

© *Sheffield Super Bowl*

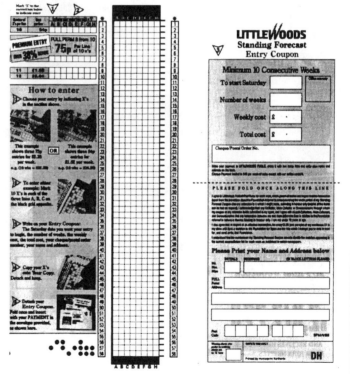

© *Littlewoods Pools*

Example

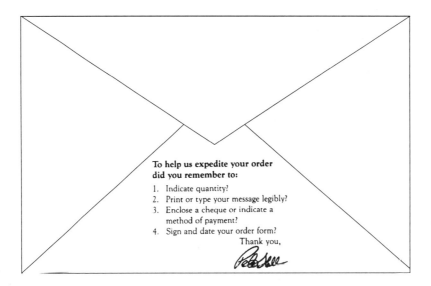

To help us expedite your order
did you remember to:

1. Indicate quantity?
2. Print or type your message legibly?
3. Enclose a cheque or indicate a
   method of payment?
4. Sign and date your order form?

Thank you,

© Adler Manufacturing

Example

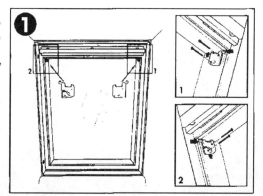

❶ English: Fix roller blind brackets to top of sash sides. Bracket with round hole on right side (1). Bracket with groove on left side (2). If these have been prefitted to window, proceed to step 2.

❶ Deutsch: Zubehörträger montieren, falls diese nicht schon am Fenster befestigt sind. Zubehörträger mit Loch: Rechte Seite (1). Zubehörträger mit Schlitz: Linke Seite (2).

❶ Français: Mettre en place les fixations du store sur la fenêtre si le modèle n'est pas équipé d'origine. Fixation avec trous: côté droit. Fixation avec rainure, côté gauche (2).

❶ Dansk: Tilbehørsbeslag monteres, hvis vinduet ikke i forvejen er forsynet med sådanne. Beslag med hul: Højre side (1). Beslag med spor: Venstre side (2).

❶ Nederlands: Monteer de bevestigingsmiddelen voor de accessoires, indien het venster daarvan nog niet is voorzien. Bevestigingsmiddel met gat: rechter zijde. Bevestigingsmiddel met sleuf: linker zijde (2).

❶ Italiano: Installare le ecche di fissaggio se la finestra e stata fornita senza. Placca con foro: ore destra (1). Placca con scanalatura: lato sinistro (2).

❶ Español: Instale os soportes de accesorios si la ventana no os tiene ya instalados. Soporte con orificio: Lado derecho (1). Soporte con ranura: Lado izquierdo (2).

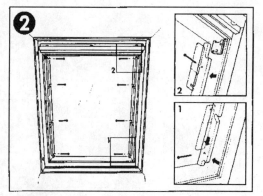

❷ English: Fit matched side sections against sash bottom (1), using key supplied to set a distance to glass (1+2).

❷ Deutsch: Rollkasten an unteres Flügelholz halten (1), mit beiliegendem Schlüssel Abstand vor Glas zu Rollenkasten festlegen (1+2).

❷ Français: Positionner les crémaillères latérales contre la traverse basse de l'ouvrant (1), utiliser le gabarit pour déterminer la distance entre le vitrage et les éléments – crémaillère – (1+2).

❷ Dansk: Gliklister monteres mod underrammen (1). Afstand mellem glas og gliklister bestemmes ved hjælp af nøglen (1+2).

❷ Nederlands: Monteer de gekoepelde zijgeleiders tegen het onderdorpelraam (1); Gebruik het zijgeleider-sleutel voor het bepalen van de afstand tussen zijgeleiders en glas (1+2).

❷ Italiano: Installare istello con ganci aderente alla parte inferiore de battente (1) usando il distanziatore per fissare la distanza fra il vetro e l'istello (1+2).

❷ Español: Coloque los listones con muescas contra la parte inferior (1). Utilice la llave para determinar la distancia entre el cristal y los listones (1+2).

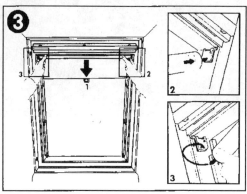

❸ English: Fit roller blind into brackets. Round pin to right side (2). Square pin firmly into groove at left (3).

❸ Deutsch: Rollo in Zubehörträger einhängen. Runde Stift des Rollos rechts (2), abgewinkelter Stift links (3) einführen.

❸ Français: Installer l'enrouleur. Côté droit ebauture: embout cylindrique dans le logement de la fixation (2). Côté gauche insérer la languette rectangulaire dans la rainure de la fixation (3).

❸ Dansk: Rullegardinet placeres. Højre side: Stiften anbringes i hul (2). Venstre side: tosetappen drejes hen i bund i sporet (3).

❸ Nederlands: Plaats het rolgordijn in. Rechter zijde: pen in gat (2). Linker zijde: gebogen as-einde in de sleuf drukken (3).

❸ Italiano: Installare il rotokante. Lato destro: il perno nel foro (2). Lato sinistro: calcare la scanalatura a scatto (3).

❸ Español: Introduzca la cortina de resorte en os soportes. Lado derecho: inserte la pieza redonda en el orificio (2). Lado izquierdo: Deslice la pieza pono en la ranura sujerando la cortina (3).

© *The Velux Company Ltd.*

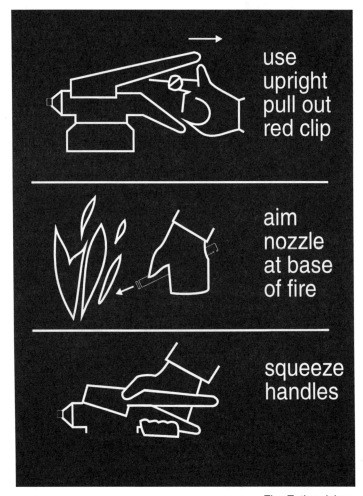

Fire Extinguisher

Example

To do	A B C	Done

Action Pad   Date:

First
- List all things to do
- Decide priorities

Next
- Link with your diary
- Transfer Today's to dos
- Don't over schedule
- Be flexible-allow for interruptions
- Group similar activities

Then
- Start with As not Cs
- Handle paper once
- Keep interruptions short

Finally
- Review your day
- Plan for tomorrow

Speak/Write to:

Don't forget:

© *Royal Life*

Use the power of graphics in your designs

The best statistical graphic?

Charles Joseph Minard (1781-1870) showed the devastating losses suffered in Napoleon's Russian campaign of 1812. Beginning at the left on the Polish-Russian border, the thick band shows the size of the army. In September the army reached Moscow, which by then was sacked and deserted, with 100 000 men. The path of Napoleon's retreat is shown by the darker, lower band, which is linked to the temperature scale and dates at the bottom of the chart. It was a bitterly cold winter, and many froze on the march out of Russia. The army finally struggled back into Poland with only 10 000 men.

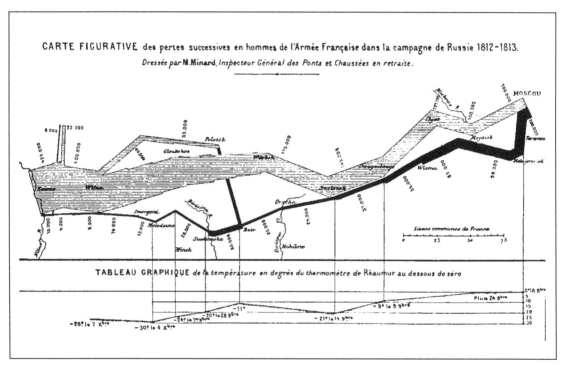

© Edward R. Tufte, *The Visual Display of Quantitative Information*
(Cheshire, Connecticut: Graphics Press, 1983)

This may be the best statistical graphic ever drawn, and shows how information can be more effectively transferred by graphics rather than text. Remember it when you come to design your pages and performance aids.

Pros and cons of different media

Now that you have a learning map, divided into modules, you have enough information to select the appropriate medium and instructional method for each module.

This makes a nonsense of all those requests for 'a CBT course' or 'a video course on...'. You will always have a mixture of media. And you can use the advantages of some media to overcome the disadvantages of others.

You probably know most of them already. Make a note of the pros and cons of the following types of media and instructional methods.

Media	Advantages	Disadvantages
1. Classroom instruction		
2. On-the-job training		
3. Books		
4. Video		

Media	Advantages	Disadvantages
5. Simulation		
6. Practical workshop		
7. Text-based Open Learning		
8. CBT		
9. Interactive video		
10. Multimedia		

Media	Advantages	Disadvantages
11. **The real thing**		
12. **Audio**		

Any more? List them here, then compare your list with ours.

Answers

Media	Advantages	Disadvantages
1. Classroom instruction	Very flexible and economical. A skilled trainer can prepare a course very quickly and can cope with many different students. Can be interactive.	Variable quality, totally dependent on the skill of the trainer. Run at the pace of the trainer, not the trainee. Encourages a teacher - student dependency. May not be interactive.
2. On-the-job training	Can be best if the trainee gets gradual practice and feedback on real issues.	Totally dependent on the quality of supervision. Can be an excuse for doing nothing.
3. Books	Flexible, portable, economical, random access, allows note-taking, self-paced. Most students are familiar with use, permanent.	Depends on the study skills and motivation of the student. Essentially passive, with no mastery of objectives before a student can continue.
4. Video	Visual impact, shows movement. Can be used for large audiences. People like watching video. Can cover an enormous amount of information. Good at presenting a message with impact.	A passive medium over which the student has no control. No testing of understanding. Conveys enormous amounts of information. Can be too entertaining. Very expensive, involves many specific skills: script-writing, filming, audio, acting, etc.
5. Simulation	Allows practice and learning on something like the real thing, if the latter is too dangerous or expensive. Can be realistic and interesting. Involves interaction. Can be computer based.	Expensive. Better to use the real thing if safety and cost not critical, e.g. software packages with training data.
6. Practical workshop	Allows interactivity. Can test the students' understanding by practical exercises. Allows discussion, questions and feedback. Cheap and flexible.	Dependent on the skill of the instructor. Good exercises take time to design. Can be difficult to run as students learn at different speeds.

Answers

Media	Advantages	Disadvantages
7. Text-based Open Learning	Cheap, flexible, self-paced. Allows access at the students' 'pace and place'. All the advantages of books plus exercises to test understanding and interact with other media.	Depends on the quality of the design. Can be patronizing. Not fully interactive.
8. CBT	Consistent, cost-effective delivery to large audience. Can be interactive. Can involve testing to check understanding. Can manage other learning media and activities. Self-paced.	Needs large audiences to justify the cost. Totally dependent on the quality of the design.
9. Interactive video	The advantages of video plus the interactivity and testing of CBT.	Very expensive, difficult to produce, modify and deliver. Only large applications can justify the cost. Totally dependent on the skills of the designers and video producers. Involves all the skills and roles of CBT + video production!
10. Multimedia	All the advantages of CBT, video plus sound, plus high quality photographs and fast reference to enormous amounts of data through CD-ROM.	Just because it can do everything does not mean you need it. Very expensive.
11. The real thing	Very relevant, cheap.	People do not necessarily learn from experience and they may learn the wrong things.
12. Audio	Can simulate audio-based performance such as radio/ telephone techniques, languages. Cheap, portable. Student can control by switching off. Study on the move, e.g. in a car.	Generally passive. No note-taking. Learners' attention 'wanders' after a few minutes.

How did your list compare with ours?

The principal lessons are:

- There is no such thing as a one-medium course, e.g. a CBT course; effective instruction always uses a mixture of media
- Use the strengths of one medium and compensate for the weaknesses in others
- Use the medium which is as close to the real thing as possible

Examples

A video	to get over a message and visual impact, e.g. selling the benefits of a training package
A workbook (text)	for the student to keep, refer to and make notes on
Computer-based testing	to test a student's understanding before he or she progresses
Practical workshops	to allow practical experience, discussion, questions, feedback, etc.

Other influences on your choice will include:

- the learner's preference
- realistic constraints, e.g. cost and time
- what you are best equipped to use
- what would please the most people with the minimum effort

Remember:

The first principle of choosing a medium is to select the one which is as close to the real thing as you can possibly get. So if the performance involves interpreting forms with handwritten data then use example forms with handwritten data, ***not*** computer simulations of forms. If the performance involves operating equipment, your final objective will have to involve that equipment.

Although it is nonsense to talk about a one-medium course, e.g. an Open Learning course, you are lucky because Open Learning is an approach rather than a method, and a general term that covers many things, including multimedia, CBT and workbooks.

Even a computer-aided lesson should have a workbook for reference and note-taking.

Finally ...

Using this book is not the best method for learning how to design effective Open Learning. This is a skill that needs practice and feedback. You can learn the essential knowledge here but you will not become skilled until you have applied that knowledge and obtained feedback. That is why we recommend that you work with an experienced colleague or supervisor.

Now that you know something about different types of media, look at your pyramid again and check your grouping of topics into modules. Do they make sense in terms of things that can conveniently be learnt together, e.g. similar methods, a skills workshop?

In our example we have added the units to the learning map because they include different types of learning which will need different media.

When you have done this for your pyramid, modify your learning map and annotate it with all the media to be used for each module or unit.

You can see from our example that a large variety of methods are used and that you frequently have options. Real constraints will probably lead you to compromise, e.g. if you cannot afford video for module 4, and you are already using CBT for 3.2 and 5, you may well end up with a CBT simulation of 4. As long as it does not detract from the learner achieving the objectives, it will be easier for you to develop and may be easier for the learner to manage.

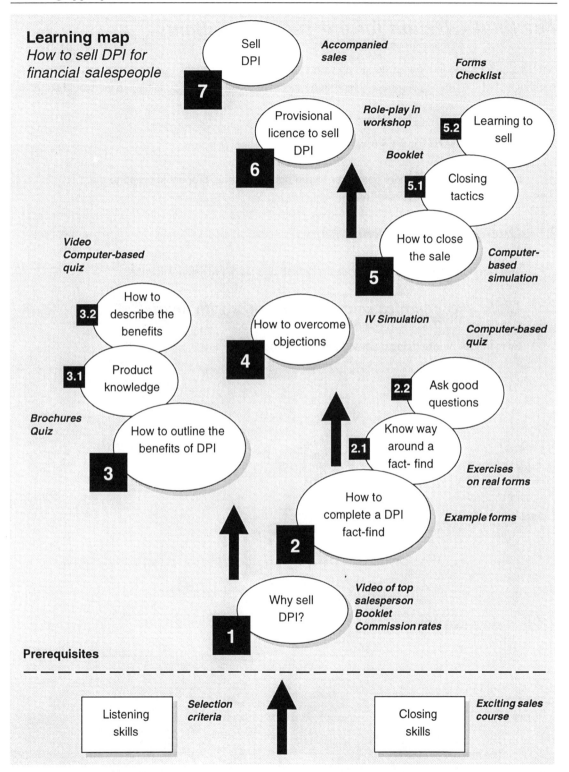

The final selection for our sales consultants

In this case we know that our target group wants to learn in short chunks and has multimedia. However, the final test of the training is probably best done as close to 'real life' as possible, so we would suggest:

1.   Open Learning package

including workbook, video, computer-based quizzes, forms, product knowledge brochures, interactive video (IV)

2.   One-day role-play workshops

with video feedback and skilled salespeople to acquire a provisional licence

3.   Eight accompanied sales in six months with debrief

by manager before being awarded full licence to sell DPI

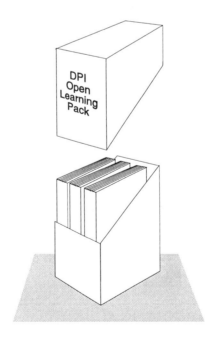

Quiz

---

1. **Have you made a list of performance aids used in everyday life?**

    No

    Yes

2. **What are three of the four main reasons for use of performance aids?**

    1.

    2.

    3.

3. **From our list of advantages and disadvantages, what is the following training medium?**

    Advantages

    *Can be best if the trainee gets
    gradual practice and feedback on
    real issues*

    Disadvantages

    *Totally dependent on the quality
    of supervision. Can be an
    excuse for doing nothing*

Quiz

4. **Have you made a list of advantages and disadvantages of different types of media?**

    No

    Yes

5. **What does effective instruction always involve?**

Answers

1. Have you made a list of performance aids used in everyday life?

No   →

Yes   ↓

2. What are three of the four main reasons for use of performance aids?

1.	To jog memory

2.	To improve information

3.	To reduce complexity

4.	To identify something quickly

3. From our list of advantages and disadvantages, what is the following training medium?

Advantages

Can be best if the trainee gets gradual practice and feedback on real issues

Disadvantages

Totally dependent on the quality of supervision. Can be an excuse for doing nothing

On-the-job training

Answers

4. **Have you made a list of advantages and disadvantages of different types of media?**

No   ➡   Go on and do so now.

Yes   ⬇   This will help you choose the best mix of
                        media for your projects.

5. **What does effective instruction always involve?**

A mixture of media

Unit 4

Starting the detailed design

Now you have broken down the topic into modules and units

- Where do you start?
- How do you give it some structure?

Objective

> *By the end of this unit you will be able to list the essential elements of a learning unit*

Follow the steps in the unit and you will know that any module you design is well structured.

Quiz

1. **You have probably designed something before; a lesson or a learning module. Assuming that you already have a design objective, what would you do next?**

2. **How would you structure the module?**

Answers

1. **You have probably designed something before; a lesson or a learning module. Assuming that you already have a design objective, what would you do next?**

The next thing you do is to design the test or quiz.

When you have a measurable objective and an appropriate test, everything that you design to go in between must be relevant to both, or it doesn't go in!

This is the way to make your designs short and relevant

You do not start by research on writing content.

Keep away from those books!

2. **How would you structure the module?**

State the performance objectives
so that the learner can visualize him or herself doing it

Sell the benefits
of doing it. You have a good idea of what motivates your students from your target group description

Check any prerequisites
so that people do not waste their time

Test existing competence

Offer learning activities for new skills and knowledge
or an option to take a test

Model the desired performance
give examples of the desired performance

Provide practice and feedback
make the exercises gradually more complex with decreasing help

Test that the learner can achieve the objective

Example of how to structure Module 1 'Why sell DPI?'

State the performance objective

Given the video and current commission rate booklet, make a commitment to complete the course, work out potential commission and benefits to you so that the commission test is +/- 5% accurate and you sign a commitment to training form

Sell the benefits

Video of top sales consultant describing benefits, standing next to her Ferrari

Check any prerequisites

Check that the learner had achieved minimum sales of normal insurance in previous six months

Test existing competence

Quiz on questioning skills

Offer learning activities

Open Learning booklet and exercises on possible commission and benefits to you

Model the desired performance

List of top sales consultants who have already made a commitment

Provide practice and feedback

Not needed

Test

Quiz on commission. Training commitment form to be signed

Project activity

Think about your project. Choose an easy module or unit and draft out how you will structure it.

State the performance objective

Sell the benefits

Check any prerequisites

Test existing competence

Offer learning activities

Model the desired performance

Provide practice and feedback

Test

Quiz

1. **When starting to design a module, given the design objective what do you do next?**

2. **What are the essential elements of any learning unit?**

Answers

1. **When starting to design a module, given the design objective, what do you do next?**

   Design the test

2. **What are the elements of any learning unit?**

   - *State the performance objectives*
   - *Sell the benefits*
   - *Check any prerequisites*
   - *Test existing competence*
   - *Offer learning activities for new skills and knowledge*
   - *Model the desired performance*
   - *Provide practice and feedback*
   - *Test that the learner can achieve the objective*

Unit 5

Test question design

Any form of training needs to include plenty of questions to test the learners' understanding before they continue. This is particularly true of CBT, interactive video and multimedia, when the computer needs to know what to show the learner next.

In designing good learning materials you will write lots of questions. This unit shows you how.

Objective

> **By the end of this unit you will be able to:**
>
> *state the most important feature of any test question*
>
> *name the three ways that tests are used*
>
> *describe how to design a question*
>
> *name six rules for designing multiple-choice questions*

Introduction

A good interactive lesson needs questions because this is the way the student is asked to think about or do something.

Questions don't come out of thin air!

They come directly from the standard part of your design objective.

So, after you have written your objective, go straight on to design the questions that make up your test. This ensures that the content of your lesson is directly relevant to your objective.

Quiz

How much do you know already?
(an example of questions being used as a learning activity)

1. What are the main ways that tests are used?

2. How do you design a question?

Answers

How much do you know already?

(an example of questions being used as a learning activity)

1. **What are the main ways that tests are used?**

   > 1. As a learning activity like this one
   > 2. To check understanding
   > 3. To test mastery

3. **How do you design a question?**

   > *Directly from the standards in your design objective*

Lesson structure and question design

The most difficult questions to design are those that will be judged by computer. This is because they have to be so specific. There are four main question types used in CBT, interactive video and multimedia:

- multiple choice
- alternative response
- matching
- free format

Multiple-choice questions

These present a problem and a series of possible responses, e.g.:

> **Which of the following is a fruit?**
>
> a. potato   ☐
> b. raspberry ☐
> c. carrot   ☐   *(choose one option)*

The advantage of multiple choice questions is that it is easy for the computer to match single key entries.

The disadvantage is that the questions are difficult to write well because suitable wrong choices (distractors) are often hard to find and the question gives many 'clues' to the student.

Alternative-response questions

These give the learner a choice of only two responses.

They are fast to respond to and can reflect realistic occasions when learners are asked to judge a statement as being right or wrong.

They only cover small pieces of information and encourage people to guess.

Prostitution is legal

True ☐

or

False ☐   **(tick the appropriate box)**

Matching questions

These present several 'premises' and possible 'responses'.

Match the codes to their correct types:

Description	**Term**
1. POST CODE	165HB
2. SHORT CODE	B1LST
3. LOCAL MLO CODE	RH12 32E
4. EXTRACT CODE	R2
	SW1

A lot of information can be included without needing much testing time.

They are hard to design.

Free-format questions

Type in your answer

> ....

➕ Good for specific answers

➖ A very dangerous type, because it is hard to match all the possible right responses, especially in CBT, and there is a danger of giving inappropriate feedback.
It is best to use free format where there is only one answer. It is better if this is a number rather than a word, e.g.: What is the melting point of steel?.................°C

The six rules for designing multiple-choice questions

You have probably taken enough multiple-choice tests to have found ways of improving your chances.

Many questions give unintentional clues. There are six rules to follow to help avoid this:

1. Make sure the question tests the real performance
2. Present a clear problem
3. Use plausible choices
4. Avoid negatives in questions
5. Avoid 'none' or 'all' in questions
6. Avoid clues

Quiz

What is wrong with the following multiple-choice questions?

---

1. **John Kennedy:**

    a.   Served as ambassador to Britain during the Second World War
    b.   Served as the thirty-fifth president of the United States of America
    c.   Served as the national chairman of the United Fund campaign
    d.   Served as the president of the United States Senate

2. **The increased speed was caused by an:**

    a.   Additive
    b.   Faulty support
    c.   Small fitting
    d.   Stone

3. **Which of the following is not an effective hangover cure?**

    a.   Hanging upside down
    b.   Drinking a lot of water the night before
    c.   Aspirin
    d.   Hair of the dog

4. **How many horses were there in the 1989 Grand National?**

    a.   12
    b.   104
    c.   42
    d.   365

Answers

> 1. This does not present a clear problem, and not enough of the item is included in the question.

> 2. A clue to the correct answer is given in the question; 'an' suggests that the correct answer is 'Additive'.

> 3. There is a negative in the question.

> 4. Not all the choices are plausible and it would be better to use ascending or descending numerical order.

The seven rules for designing matching questions

There are seven rules for good design of matching questions:

1. Make sure it tests the real performance
2. Include clear directions for what the learner needs to do
3. Keep the items homogeneous
4. Make all the matches plausible
5. Offer more responses than premises
6. Keep responses shorter than premises
7. Use logical order

Some common errors

Directions: place the letter to the left of each number. Use each letter only once.

1.	*91*
2.	*Carburettor*
3.	*Spark plug*
4.	*Windscreen*
5.	*V-12*

a.	*Engine with 12 cylinders*
b.	*Mixes air with petroleum*
c.	*Ignites fuel*
d.	*Protects driver from wind*
e.	*Measures engine size*
f.	*An octane rating*

These are premises   **These are responses**

What is wrong with the example?

- Each premise should relate to an engine part or a type of engine, but not to both
- Item 1 does not match feasibly with any alternatives except f
- Items are better arranged in numerical or alphabetical order

A better example

Directions: *Write the letter of the automobile part to the left of its function.*
             Not all the letters are used.

Function

1.	*Mixes petroleum and air*
2.	*Assists in cooling*
3.	*Protects driver from dirt particles*
4.	*Recharges battery*

Automobile part

a.	*Alternator*
b.	*Carburettor*
c.	*Radiator*
d.	*Spark plug*
e.	*Windscreen*

How are questions used in Open Learning?

- To allow the learner to learn by discovery, e.g. by asking 'How much do you know already?'

- To test a learner's understanding before he or she progresses, e.g. by using a quiz

- To test achievement of the standards for the objective, e.g. by using module tests or unit tests, sometimes called 'criterion tests'

Remember!

People are afraid of tests, so use terms like 'quiz' or 'check yourself' and make it clear which are quizzes and which are criterion tests.

Example

Test for Module 1 'Why sell DPI?'

The test questions always come from the objective:

Given	Module 1, video and booklet containing commission notes
Performance	Make a commitment to do the course to obtain a licence to sell DPI, work out potential commission and benefits to you
Standard	Commission +/- 5% accurate
Method of assessment	Signed commitment

So appropriate questions are:

✓/✗

1. **Have you completed the exercise on identifying the benefits to you?** ☐

2. **Did you pass the commission quiz within +/- 5% of the correct answers?** ☐

3. **Have you signed the commitment form to do the course?** ☐

Practice

Take an objective from your unit and write a test question.

Show it to a colleague.

Does it answer the questions on page 169?

Checklist

Does your test question:

✓

- **come from the standards in your design objective?** ☐

- **relate to the desired performance?** ☐

- **present a clear problem?** ☐

- **avoid unintentional clues?** ☐

- **test what you want it to test?** ☐

Quiz

1. **What is the most important feature of any test question?**

2. **In what ways are tests used?**

3. **How do you design a test or question?**

4. **What are the six rules for designing multiple-choice questions?**

1.

2.

3.

4.

5.

6.

Answers

1. **What is the most important feature of any test question?**

    > **That it is relevant to performance**

2. **In what ways are tests used?**

    > 1.   **As a learning activity**
    > 2.   **To test understanding**
    > 3.   **To check mastery**

3. **How do you design a test or question?**

    > **Look at the standards part of your design objectives**

4. **What are the six rules for designing multiple-choice questions?**

    > 1.   **Make sure the question tests the real performance**

    > 2.   **Present a clear problem**

    > 3.   **Use plausible choices**

    > 4.   **Avoid negatives in questions**

    > 5.   **Avoid 'none' or 'all' in questions**

    > 6.   **Avoid unintentional clues, e.g. answers of a different length**

How to Design
Effective Open Learning

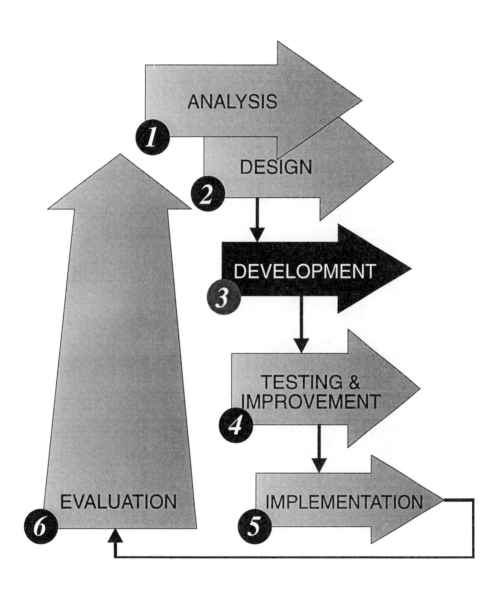

Module 3

Module 3 Development

- ***Unit 1***

Clear, effective writing

- ***Unit 2***

Page design

- ***Unit 3***

Screen design for CBT and multimedia

- ***Unit 4***

Programmer ready material

Unit 1

Clear, effective writing

Objective

By the end of this unit you will be able to:

name five guidelines for making your text readable

demonstrate six examples of poor writing that you have rewritten in an active, personal style

find a copy of suggested text standards

Content is more important than presentation!

Page design cannot be considered in isolation. If your instructional design is poor, then no amount of effective presentation will make it effective. A key part of presentation is *clear, effective writing* that is appropriate to your target group. You have already seen that the more you can 'get into the shoes' of the target group the better you can design effective materials.

Working with high performers and writing down what they say, in the way they say it, will also make your writing lively and appropriate. A key skill of design at this stage is how you write in the *active, personal style* rather than the passive, formal language often used by experts.

An example of passive formal language

Here is an extract from an accounting textbook:

THE COMPANIES ACT

The accounting provisions introduced in the successive Companies Acts have not for the most part had the effect of forcing additional disclosures by most companies, but of bringing the minority of 'laggards' up to the standard of the majority.

The most basic effect of legal provisions is that accounts are publicly available for all companies. Every company must deliver a copy of its accounts to the Registrar of Companies for filing in publicly available files. The Companies Act 1976, sections 1-6, has tightened up the regulations for filing so that the accounts available in a company's files should no longer be out of date as they have been hitherto. In practice, public companies will always send a copy of their latest annual report and accounts to anyone who requests it.

You do not have to write like this.

If you take out the redundant information and use the active voice and personal style, you could present all the above information like this:

How to analyse other companies' accounts

Every public company must file a recent copy with the Registrar of Companies. Another good source is simply to ring the company concerned and ask for a copy.

If you are filing a copy, check the Companies Act 1976 (sections 1-6) for the regulations.

Which would you rather read?

Notice how all the same information is included in the second version.

Some guidelines for readability

- Write for your target group

- Use the active voice (subject, verb, object)

- Make it personal: 'You ...'

- Use short sentences

- Cut out redundant information

- Keep it concise!

- Use short sentences

- Link with graphics

- Get someone to criticize it

- Use headings to convey information actively, e.g.: 'How to ...'

Quiz

Rewrite the following in a more active and interesting way.

1. None of the above was understood by anyone.

2. Open Learning Demonstration

This booklet that you are about to read consists of short extracts of Open Learning produced for the MOG Fighter project. This project has been commissioned by the Borlandic Air Force to assist in the training of their pilots and weapon system operators.

3. Busyness

One of the escape mechanisms from job-induced anxiety is the development of time-consuming activities that managers find less threatening to perform than the innovative or tough aspects of their job. This is labelled busyness.

Quiz

4. **Notice to all visitors**

    Will all visitors refrain from requesting to deposit luggage in reception.

5. **'This is the chief steward speaking. Will all passengers please note that the buffet car will be closing in 10 minutes. Will any passengers requiring refreshments during this time please come to the buffet car. The buffet is situated between first and standard class at the front of the train.'**

6. **This way to the fish shop.**

Answers

Rewrite the following in a more active and interesting way.

1. *None of the above was understood by anyone.*

> *No one understood it*

2. *Open Learning Demonstration*

> *This booklet that you are about to read consists of short extracts of Open Learning produced for the MOG Fighter project. This project has been commissioned by the Borlandic Air Force to assist in the training of their pilots and weapon system operators.*

> *MOG Fighter Project - Open Learning Demonstration Booklet*

3. *Busyness*

> *One of the escape mechanisms from job-induced anxiety is the development of time-consuming activities that managers find less threatening to perform than the innovative or tough aspects of their job. This is labelled busyness.*

> *Busyness*
>
> *One escape from job-induced anxiety is to do things*
> *that are less threatening than new or tough parts of a job.*

Answers

4. Notice to all visitors

Will all visitors refrain from requesting to deposit luggage in reception.

Sorry, we cannot keep your luggage in reception.

5. 'This is the chief steward speaking. Will all passengers please note that the buffet car will be closing in 10 minutes. Will any passengers requiring refreshments during this time please come to the buffet car. The buffet is situated between first and standard class at the front of the train.'

'The buffet will be open for another 10 minutes.'

Performance aids showing direction to the buffet car

6. This way to the fish shop.

Unit 2

Page design

Objective

By the end of this unit you will be able to:

- state five lessons of good page design for Open Learning

- state the recommended minimum number of typefaces to use

- name four types of page in a skeleton lesson

Exercise

Get hold of some Open Learning materials.

• What layouts do you like?

• What layouts don't you like?

Here are some examples to get you started:

Example

Dolore: te feugait nulla facilisi. Nam liber tempor cum soluta nobis eleifend option congue nihil imperdiet doming id quod mazim placerat facer possim
Lorem: ipsum dolor sit amet, consectetuer adipiscing elit, sed diam nonummy nibh euismod tincidunt ut
Laoreet: dolore magna aliquam erat volutpat. Ut wisi

DELENIT AUGUE DUIS DOLORE TE FEUGAIT

Enim: ad minim veniam, quis nostrud exerci tation ullamcorper suscipit lobortis nisl ut aliquip ex ea
Vel: illum dolore eu feugiat nulla facilisis at vero eros et
Accumsan: et iusto odio dignissim qui blandit praesent luptatum zzril delenit augue duis dolore te feugait nulla facilisi. Lorem ipsum dolor sit amet, consectetuer adipiscing elit, sed diam nonummy nibh euismod
Tincidunt ut laoreet dolore magna aliquam erat.

Ut wisi enim ad minim veniam, quis nostrud exerci

Tation: ullamcorper suscipit lobortis nisl ut aliquip ex ea commodo consequat. Duis autem vel eum iriure dolor in hendrerit in vulputate velit esse molestie consequat,
Vel: illum dolore eu feugiat nulla facilisis at vero eros et
Accumsan: et iusto odio dignissim qui blandit praesent luptatum zzril delenit augue duis dolore te feugait nulla
Facilisi: Lorem ipsum dolor sit amet, consectetuer

ADIPISCING ELIT, SED DIAM

Nonummy: nibh euismod *tincidunt* ut laoreet dolore *magna* aliquam erat volutpat. Ut wisi *enim* ad minim
Veniam: quis nostrud exerci tation ullamcorper suscipit

Example

■ Et iusto odio

Lorem ipsum dolor sit amet, consectetuer adipiscing elit, sed diam nonummy nibh euismod tincidunt ut laoreet dolore magna

Aliquam erat volutpat. Ut wisi enim ad minim

Veniam, quis nostrud exerci tation

1.	
2.	
3.	

Lorem ipsum:

- Ullamcorper suscipit lobortis nisl ut aliquip ex ea commodo consequat. Duis autem vel eum

- iriure dolor in
- hendrerit in
- vulputate velit

■ Accumsan

Esse molestie consequat?

vel - vel illum dolore
eu - eu feugiat nulla facilisis at vero eros et

Eu feugiat nulla facilisis at 1

21

Example

Incidunt 3

Dolore magna

Dignissim qui blandit praesent luptatum zzril delenit augue duis dolore te feugait nulla facilisi. Lorem ipsum dolor sit amet,

> Consectetuer adipiscing elit, sed diam nonummy nibh euismod tincidunt ut laoreet

1 _____
2 _____
3 _____

aliquam erat volutpat.

- ad minim veniam
- quis nostrud exerci tation
- ullamcorper suscipit

Ut wisi enim

lobortis nisl ut aliquip ex ea commodo consequat. Duis autem vel eum iriure dolor in hendrerit in vulputate velit esse molestie

consequat, vel illum dolore eu feugiat nulla facilisis at vero eros et accumsan et iusto odio dignissim qui blandit praesent luptatum

1 _____
2 _____
3 _____

Example

9. Obortis nisl ut aliquip ex ea commodo consequat. Duis autem vel eum iriure dolor in hendrerit in vulputate

(a) Velit esse molestie consequat, vel illum dolore eu feugiat nulla facilisis at vero eros et accumsan et iusto odio dignissim qui blandit praesent luptatum zzril delenit augue duis
- Dolore te feugait nulla facilisi. Lorem ipsum dolor
- Sit amet, consectetuer
- Adipiscing elit, sed diam
- Nonummy nibh euismod tincidunt ut laoreet dolore magna aliquam erat
- Volutpat. Ut wisi enim ad
- Minim veniam, quis nostrud exerci tation ullamcorper
- Suscipit lobortis nisl ut
- aliquip ex ea commodo consequat. Duis autem vel eum iriure dolor in hendrerit
- In vulputate velit esse molestie consequat, vel
- Illum dolore eu feugiat nulla facilisis at vero eros et
- Accumsan et iusto odio dignissim qui blaobortis nisl
- Ut aliquip ex ea commodo consequat. Duis autem vel
- Eum iriure dolor in hendrerit
- In vulputate velit esse molestie consequat, vel
- Illum dolore eu feugiat nulla.

- lobortis nisl ut aliquip ex ea commodo
- consequat. Duis autem
(b) Vel eum iriure dolor in hendrerit in vulputate velit esse molestie consequat,
- vel illum dolore eu feugiat nulla facilisis at
- vero eros et accumsan et iusto odio dignissim
- qui blandit praesent luptatum zzril delenit
- augue duis dolore te feugait nulla facilisi. Lorem ipsum dolor sit amet, consectetuer adipiscing elit, sed diam
- nonummy nibh euismod
- tincidunt ut laoreet
- dolore magna aliquam erat volutpat. Ut wisi enim ad minim veniam, quis nostrud exerci
- tation ullamcorper suscipit lobortis nisl ut aliquip ex ea commodo
- consequat. Duis autem vel eum iriure dolor in
- hendrerit in vulputate velit esse molestie consequat, vel illum
(c) dolore te feugait nulla facilisi. Lorem ipsum dolor sit amet, consectetuer adipiscing elit, sed diam nonummy nibh euismod

Example

AUTEM

Diam 2   **Lorem ipsum dolor sit amet**

2.5   Consectetuer adipiscing elit?

sed diam nonummy nibh euismod tincidunt ut laoreet dolore magna aliquam erat volutpat. Ut wisi enim ad **minim.**

nostrud exerci tation

ullamcorper suscipit lobortis nisl ut aliquip ex ea commodo.

- Duis autem vel
- eum iriure dolor
- in hendrerit in
- vulputate velit esse

molestie

Dignissim qui blandit praesent luptatum

- consectetuer (ADIPISCING) elit
- sed diam nonummy (NIBH) euismod
- tincidunt ut laoreet (*)

Consequat, vel illum dolore eu feugiat nulla facilisis.

at vero

Eros et accumsan et iusto odio.

Zzril delenit augue duis dolore te feugait nulla facilisi
Lorem ipsum dolor sit amet

192

What did you think?

Good layout is very subjective
Some of the things you may have noticed:

- Too much text can give a cramped feel to the page

- Just enough white space gives an active feel to the page

- Mix graphics, bullet points and short sentences but don't overdo it

- Use unjustified right-hand margins (they are easier to read)

- Allocate areas of the page consistently for specific purposes

- Only use graphics for a purpose

- If you are using a binder, leave a wide enough inner margin

Typefaces

You will need help in designing a style sheet for your document. For a consistent look, choose two typefaces at the most, and decide when they will be used. For this book we have used:

# Headline	Times Roman Bold 30 point
## *Subhead 1*	Times Roman Bold Italic 22 point
Subhead 2	Times Roman Bold Italic 17 point
Subhead 3	Times Roman Bold Italic 14 point
Body text	Helvetica 9 point
Emphasis	Bold italics

I recommend that you get some help from a professional designer, choose typefaces and style sheets for your house style and then stick to them.

A skeleton design

Each learning unit will have a similar structure.

You will have to decide on page layouts for:

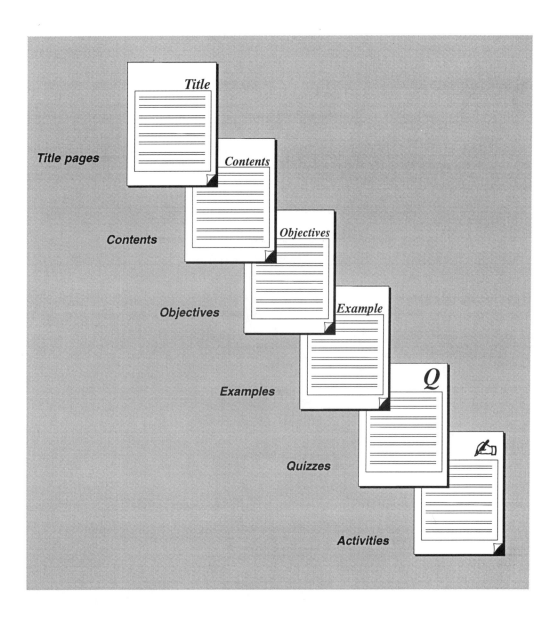

Some examples of how page layout gives the learner valuable information

Note:

1 how boxes and drop shadows always tell the reader that these are examples

2 how the action plan always has the same layout

3 how the grey backgrounds and white boxes are used when people have to fill something in

In this way the learner gets information without realizing it.

**Examples
of Vision Statements**

I.B.M.

'Our goal is simply stated.
We want to be the best

A.C.T. CONSULTANTS

'We work with you to improve
people's performance in areas vita
to the success of your business.
We design and implement the bes
training solutions so that you want
to work with us again, and we earr
a reputation for doing the best wor
in our field.

HONDA

'Quality in all jobs - learn, t
analyse, evaluate and impr
Reliable products - on time,
excellence and consistency.
communication - listen, ask
speak up.'

BUDGET TRAVEL

'Budget Travel provides econ
holiday travel and related se
to customers in the London
who expect efficient, problen
travel arrangements at low c

Action	Who	Target Date
Read this unit, draft your own Vision Statement		
Get the Chief Executive (CE) to decide whether to produce a new Vision Statement or modify an existing one		
Get the CE to decide who should be involved		
Circulate this unit to the team involved		
Get them to record their i		
Arrange a meeting to agr Vision Statement		
Find outside help if necessary		
Follow the format to agr common Vision Stateme		
Communicate the Vision Statement to all staff		

1

2

Vision Statement

To be completed by the top team.

What is the purpose of the organisation; why does it exist?	
What products and/or services do you offer?	
What makes you distinctive from your competitors?	
What do you want to overhear your customers saying about you?	
What value will you offer to your customers?	
What value will you offer to your staff?	
Write a few short sentences to summarise the above. 'Our vision statement is that...'	

*From the Business Improvement Series
Investment in People Ltd.*

3

Testing and editing

It's harder to edit in a page layout programme such as *PageMaker* or *Ventura* than in a word processor. You need an example of page layout to test with your target group, but the whole document does not have to be in this form. I recommend **producing the first complete module in finished DTP form but, if possible, leaving the rest in a good word processor.** Get your draft Open Learning material checked and tested by a high performer/subject matter expert and by representatives from your target group. Keep the number of test copies to a minimum and ask people to make comments in different coloured pens or on Post-it notes which you can transfer to your master copy.

Do all this and edit as far as possible in the word processor before you give the material to your desktop publisher. He or she will love you for it and you will save a great deal of time in producing your final document.

Quiz

1. State five lessons of good page design for Open Learning.

2. What is the recommended number of typefaces to use?

3. Name four types of page that you might have in a skeleton design.

Answers

1. **State five lessons of good page design for Open Learning.**

   - Too much text can give a cramped feel to the page
   - Just enough white space gives an active feel to the page
   - Mix graphics, bullet points and short sentences but don't overdo it
   - Use unjustified right-hand margins (they are easier to read)
   - Allocate areas of the page consistently for specific purposes
   - Only use graphics for a purpose
   - If you are using a binder, leave a big enough inner margin

2. **What is the recommended number of typefaces to use?**

   Two

3. **Name four types of page that you might have in a skeleton design.**

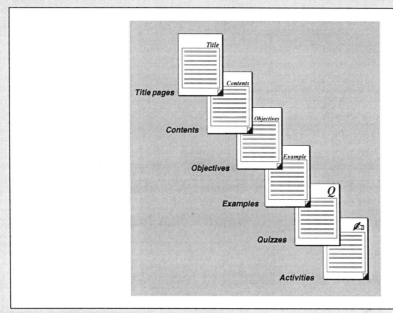

Unit 3

Screen design for CBT and multimedia

Objective

By the end of this unit you will be able to:

state the key factors to be considered in screen design

describe four general principles to aim for when using colour on the screen

describe the first secret of good screen design

complete an exercise to redesign three screens

*describe how clear design objectives help you
design interactive video*

The key facts to consider

Screen design cannot be considered in isolation. If your instructional design is poor then no amount of cosmetic presentation will save it from criticism.

The first factors to consider in any presentation are your ***audience*** and your ***objective.***

A clear idea of the needs and constraints of your ***target group*** and what you expect it to be able to do (***the desired performance***) will allow you to cut out irrelevant material and present the key learning points as interactive activities, using language that means something to the learner, rather than the sort of language that appears in manuals.

The active use of design objectives

How do we turn boring subject matter like the accountancy text you saw earlier into an interesting screen-based unit?

Remember what it started off like?

THE COMPANIES ACT

The accounting provisions introduced in the successive Companies Acts have not for the most part had the effect of forcing additional disclosures by most companies, but of bringing the minority of 'laggards' up to the standard of the majority.

The most basic effect of legal provisions is that accounts are publicly available for all companies. Every company must deliver a copy of its accounts to the Registrar of Companies for filing in publicly available files. The Companies Act 1976, sections 1-6, has tightened up the regulations for filing so that the accounts available in a company's files should no longer be out of date as they have been hitherto. In practice public companies will always send a copy of their latest annual report and accounts to anyone who requests it.

To turn this into something more active we need to know:

- who the training is for

- what they need to be able to do with this knowledge

We can then write design objectives which will actually give us our screen design and test questions.

So the first secret of good screen design is to write good design objectives.

To find out our objectives we ask our high performer:

- 'Who are the people who use this knowledge?'

- 'What do they need to know in order to ...?'

Let's assume the first answer is

> *Trainee accountants*

The answer to the second question

> *'What do they need to know?' is that 'the accounts are available for all public companies with the Registrar of Companies, or ask the company.*
>
> *You need to know the regulations for filing in the Companies Act 1976, sections 1-6.'*

This allows us to write three design objectives:

1. Given the need to analyse a company's accounts, state whether these are available to anyone.

2. Given the need to find a set of accounts, state two sources.

3. Given the need to check the regulations, state the year of the appropriate Companies Act.

We can then design three questions, add in a well written summary for remedial feedback and an opening screen and we have the outline content to go on our screens. See page 207.

Screen content and flowchart

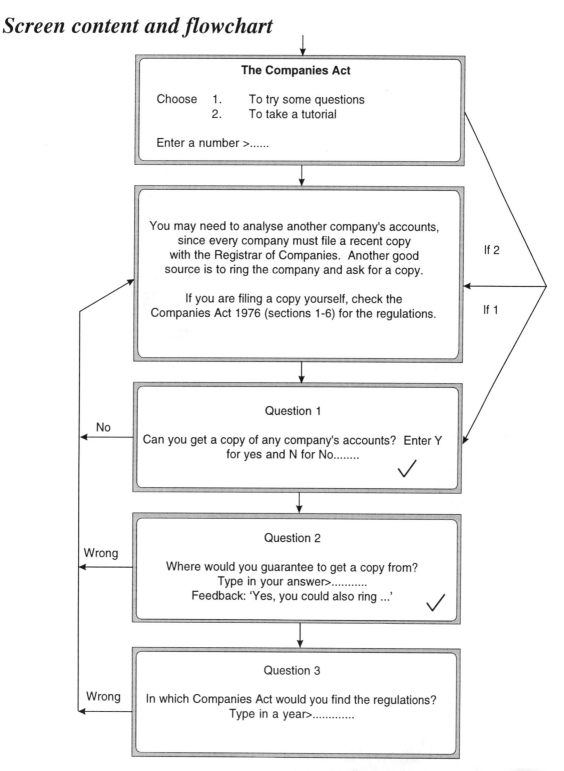

Some presentation tips...

Contrast

A key principle of attractive design is smooth contrast drop, e.g. white lettering on a black background gives too much of a drop. A little theory ...

Black makes colour and white appear more luminous.

White makes black appear more saturated and deeper.

Grey makes colour appear more colourful.

Contrasting colours stand out from each other:

* ***black and white***
* ***black and yellow***
* ***blue and white***
* ***grey and white***

Brightness

Colours also vary in brightness according to the background with which they are contrasted:

So in your screen designs go for a stepped contrast drop, i.e. black border, blue or grey background and then white lettering rather than white on black. Try it on your computer and see what you prefer.

General principles in the use of colour

Avoid:

- using colours for no particular purpose

- bright colours

- hot colours (e.g. pink and magenta appear to pulse on the screen; they are good for highlighting)

- too many colours

- non complementary colours e.g. red and yellow, green and blue

Aim for:

- consistent meanings for colours

- not more than four colours on the screen (except graphics)

- pale, pastel colours

- low-contrast background colour, such as grey

- colour contrast between character and background, e.g. white lettering on grey

- an overall style, e.g. with graded changes in contrast from background (grey?) to text (white) and highlights (red, yellow, green, pink).

Standard screen types

Just as with paper-based Open Learning there are several types of screen that you will always need, e.g.

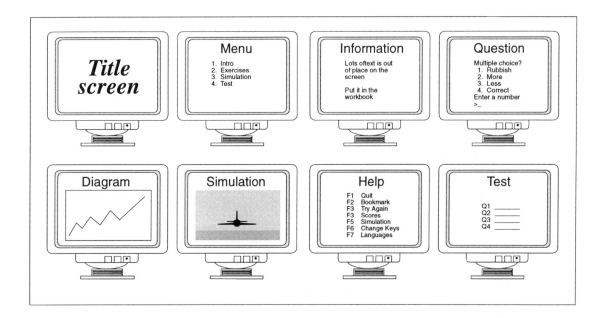

Why not produce skeleton designs for all of these?

This is especially important if you are designing as part of a large course and want to maintain a consistent 'identity'. A skeleton or standard lesson also acts as an extremely valuable performance aid for new designers.

Standard screen components

Reference information

The most common consideration for learners is 'How much is there still to do?' You can answer this by putting a module and unit name at the top of each screen and even a screen number. Use a consistent banner in a subdued colour so that it blends into the border but the learner can find it if he or she wants to, just like the way *Windows* always tells you what file you are in.

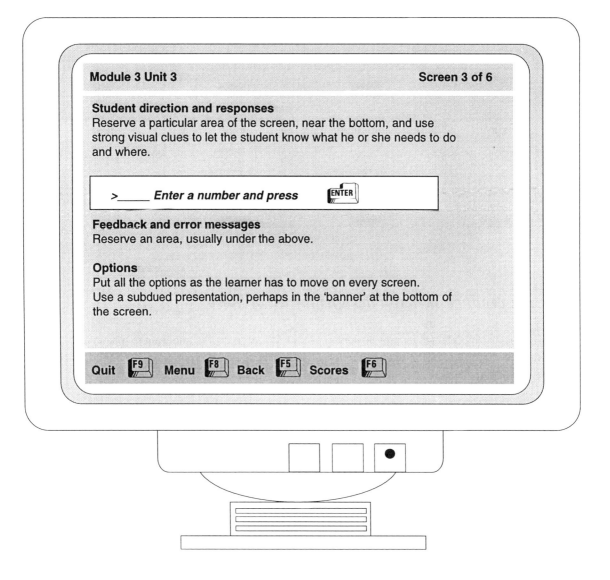

Function areas

It is a good idea to keep the screen components in function areas, e.g.:

Text and graphic areas

- Avoid text which wraps around graphics.
- Build up complex graphics in stages, perhaps with a silhouette.

Windows

Many authoring tools and word processors are *Windows*-based.

Have a look at the parts of a window and see how reference and options are always available but are unobtrusive.

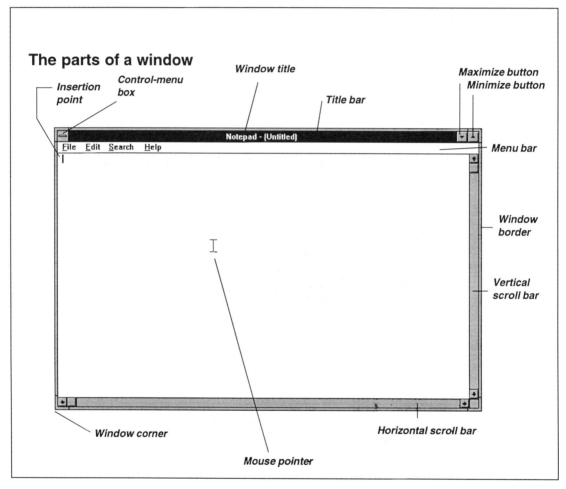

© Microsoft

Windows are designed to be used intuitively and *Microsoft Windows* is now so common that you would be well advised either to use a *Windows*-based authoring tool or make your CBT work in the same intuitive way.

If you do not already know how *Windows* works, then I suggest you get a colleague to show you now. It is probably the best example of a user-friendly screen.

Readability

You can see that the same rules about effective writing apply to text that appears on the screen but more so! People do not generally like reading from a screen. Basically, it is luminous, not reflective, and is harder to read.

A few guidelines for readable text on the screen

- Use as little text as possible

- Use short lines (like newspaper columns)

- Present text in natural blocks, not a page at a time (blank screens cost nothing, unlike paper)

- Do not indent

- Use ragged, right-hand justification, which is easier to read

- Avoid text wrapping around graphics

- Again, use as little text as possible (if there is a lot of text, put it in a workbook)

- Avoid too many fonts (no more than two)

Redesign the following real examples of screen design where little attention was given to the style of text or to the graphic power of the screen.

---

1. *If this is your first time using this style, it is recommended that you select the option 'Introduction to the system'.*

           1.   Introduction
           2.   Middle
           3.   Test

Make your selection by number or touch.

---

2. *BEACON DEMONSTRATION*

This demonstration shows the displays used to navigate a Cessna aircraft when it is being guided using a beacon.

The demonstration comprises a sequence of displays which indicate the position of the aircraft relative to the beacon, while approaching and landing on runway 5 at Heathrow.

You may stop the demonstration at any time by pressing the DATA key, and restart it by pressing the NEXT key.

Press the QUIT key to return to the menu.

Press the NEXT key to start the demonstration.

---

3. *COURSEWARE DEMONSTRATION*

The demonstration that you are about to see consists of a short sequence of courseware produced for the MOG project. The project has been commissioned by the Borlandic Air Force to assist in the training of their pilots and weapon system operators.

        Touch the screen or

        Press any key to continue

Redesign your screens here:

1

2

3

Answers

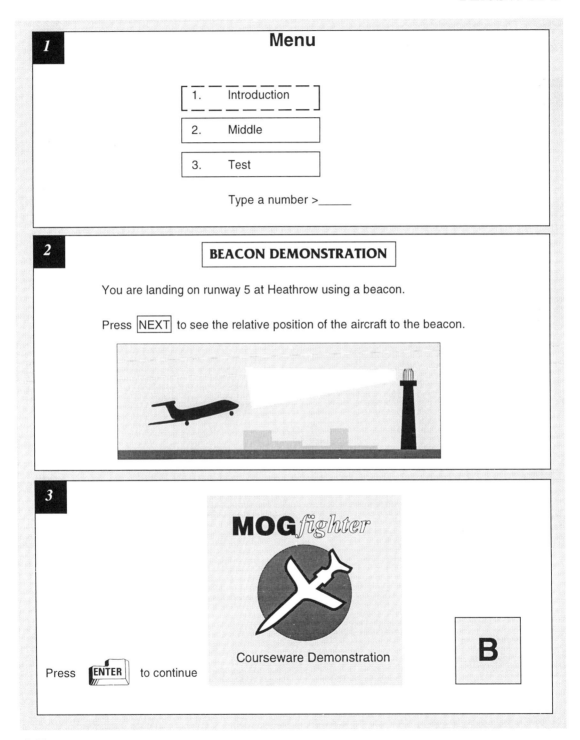

1

Menu

1.   Introduction

2.   Middle

3.   Test

Type a number >_____

2

BEACON DEMONSTRATION

You are landing on runway 5 at Heathrow using a beacon.

Press NEXT to see the relative position of the aircraft to the beacon.

3

MOGfighter

Courseware Demonstration

Press ENTER to continue

B

Screen design for interactive video

Interactive video is CBT plus video.

The same principles for screen design apply as for CBT, except that you need to decide how to present the computer-generated decisions and choices on the screen.

The most common method is to leave the frozen video as a background and superimpose a window, e.g.:

Would you:

a)   Ask another question?
b)   Offer DPI?
c)   Show him the DPI brochure?

Try to be consistent

Put the window in the same place if possible so that the learner knows where to expect it.
Look at other IVC products the learner may have seen and follow the same conventions.

Try to stick to *Windows* conventions as much as possible.

Interactive video

'A picture paints a thousand words.'

Whoever said this was absolutely right. A picture carries enormous amounts of information, and a moving one even more so. This is one of the dangers of using video for training. There is so much information being presented
, the learner can be taking in the wrong bits.

Therefore, it is important to follow a good instructional design. Write a good design objective and tell the learner what to expect (the objectives) in order to 'tune' their perception into receiving what is important.

- Let him or her 'do' the performance, e.g. by interacting with a simulation to make decisions that he or she would have to make in real life.

- Test that he or she can master the learning objectives defined at the beginning.

The principles of good interactive video design are the same as for any learning materials:

- Be clear about the desired performance
- Design for your target group
- Have clear design objectives, including conditions, performance and standards

  The **conditions** will tell you what scene to present on video, if necessary
  The **performance** tells you what the learner has to do, how he or she interacts with the computer
  The **standards** tell you how the learner, and the computer, know that the learner has mastered this part and so can move on

- Add to this clear, unobtrusive reference information as to where the learner is and flexible routeing (menus) around the material, plus
- Unfussy screen design for the computer-generated material and excellent production quality video.

Computer-based simulation

This is often overlooked as a vehicle for Open Learning but is a very effective method of learning.

One of our principles of good design is that the method you use should be as close to the real thing as possible. So what better than simulating the real performance?

SimCity © is a computer game that was designed for adults who plan how to build a city. It is so much fun that it has become a best-selling game for children and is still used on Masters courses for city planning.

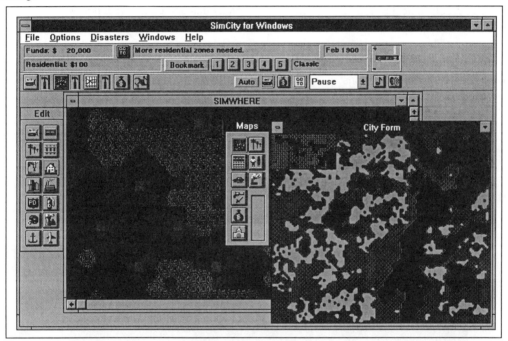

© Maxis

Notice how it uses a standard *Windows* format.

The learning comes from planning a city for real and seeing the results of your actions as you run the simulation. If you create an unhealthy environment people move out, tax revenue goes down, etc. *SimCity* is now being produced in a multimedia version, with clips of video showing the results of fires, riots and your negotiations with the mayor's office. This may seem very complex but a mainly text-based simulation may be within your grasp, see page 222.

A computer-based situation simulation

In one of ACT's Open Learning packages the design objective required the learner to spot opportunities for selling certain products during meetings with customers.

A prerequisite was a quick-reference product knowledge guide in the form of a small ring-binder showing all the products with their features and benefits.

We designed the following simulation to allow learners to:

- find which products best suited the customer's situation by trial and error in a series of simulated meetings

- test their product knowledge and ability to spot opportunities in a test versus the computer using a random set of simulations

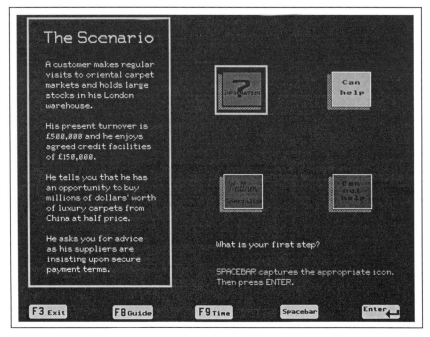

© ACT Consultants Ltd.

What is multimedia?

The screen below comes from *Musical Instruments* © *Microsoft*.

Click on the underlined words (***hot words***) and you go to further information about each topic.

Click on the sound symbol and you can hear what the instrument sounds like.

© *Microsoft*

In other parts of the program you can see clips of video, graphics, animation of high-quality still photographs, etc. See page 224 for examples.

The technology that has made all this possible is compact disc, plus adding high-quality video and sound cards to your humble PC.

The National Council for Educational Technology defines multimedia as:

'programming which combines text, audio, graphics, animation, and/or still and moving pictures. Multimedia systems integrate AV and computer resources on a single medium which may be stored on some form of compact disc (CD) or computer disk.'

Examples of multimedia

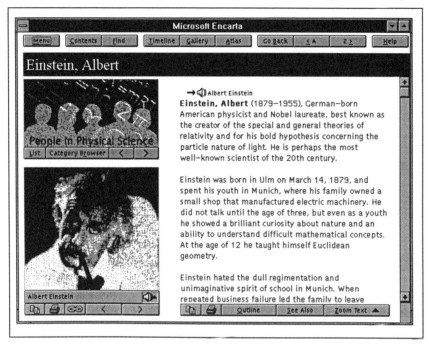

© Microsoft

© CD Sports Ltd

Screen design for multimedia

I saw some commercial multimedia the other day that had a garish brown menu screen with yellow lines all over it! The icons were colourful and novel and the whole thing looked a mess.

When we got into the lesson the material was patronizing and educational. A tutor's voice told me what 'should happen'.

The text that appeared on the screen came straight out of a textbook and would scroll down as I read it.

The small clips of video were jerky and appeared in tiny windows.

> *Just because it is multimedia don't forget the principles*
> *of good design, they aren't new!*

Whoever designed the multimedia above did not know:

- how to use colour on screen (from CBT design)
- how to keep icons, routeing and reference material unobtrusive (CBT design)
- that they could have used a *Windows*-based interface for an instant professional result
- how to focus on performance rather than knowledge
- how to rewrite text for the screen in an active, personal style

> *Multimedia is new but the fundamental design skills*
> *needed to make it effective are not.*

Good uses for multimedia

Multimedia can be used as an interactive and creative way to access information. For example, the *Musical Instruments* program allows learners to browse and discover in a very interactive way. You have all the advantages of an interactive book:

- high-quality illustrations
- flexible routeing
- clips of sound
- video

It is no accident that the first multimedia CDs are encyclopedias, and topics that need sound like music and language.

Another good use of multimedia is for language training...

...mainly because of the built-in sound facility that used to need a separate cassette player.
Now a microphone also allows you to record your responses and compare them with the pronunciation of the tutor.

Lots of good language-training materials already exist with booklets, audio and video tapes and CBT quizzes which can now be brought together.

It can also enhance CBT.

The Mavis Beacon Typing tutor is a successful CBT lesson in its own right. This is because it is a performance-based package using the real medium of the keyboard to develop skills in a challenging and fun way.

The core design qualities are nothing to do with multimedia.

However, the multimedia version has better graphics and added sound feedback that makes it appear more attractive to the learner.

Beware of entertainment and attractive displays

There is a danger that multimedia, like CBT and interactive video before it, will seduce people into thinking that just because something is more attractive it must increase the motivation of the learner.

The cosmetic part of any package will soon wear off when the learner realizes that the material is not relevant and does not help him or her do things better.

Quiz

1. Write down the first two factors to be considered when designing a screen.

    1.

    2.

2. Describe four general principles to aim for when using colour on the screen.

    1.

    2.

    3.

    4.

3. What is the first secret of good screen design?

Quiz

4. **Have you completed the screen redesign exercise (page 216)?**

    No

    Yes

5. **How do clear design objectives help you design interactive video?**

Answers

1. **Write down the first two factors to be considered when designing a screen.**

   1.   **The needs and constraints of your target group**

   2.   **The design objective**

2. **Describe four general principles to aim for when using colour on the screen.**

   Aim for:
   - *consistent meanings for colours*
   - *not more than four colours on the screen (except graphics)*
   - *pale, pastel colours*
   - *low contrast background colours, such as grey*
   - *colour-contrast between character and background, e.g. white lettering on grey*
   - *bright contrasting for diagrams and highlights, e.g. magenta or light green on grey*
   - *an overall style, e.g. with graded changes in contrast from background (grey?) to text (white) and highlights (red, yellow, green, pink)*

3. **What is the first secret of good screen design?**

   To write good design objectives

Answers

4. Have you completed the screen redesign exercise (page 216)?

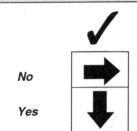

No

Yes

Go back and do it. It is a standard for this unit.

5. How do clear design objectives help you design interactive video?

- the conditions will tell you what scene to present on video, if necessary
- the performance tells you what the learner has to do, how he or she interacts with the computer
- the standards tell you how the learner, and the computer, know that the learner has mastered this bit and can move on

Unit 4

Programmer ready material

Objective

> ***By the end of this unit you will be able to:***
>
> ***draw three standard flowchart symbols***
>
> ***state what PRM stands for***
>
> ***name the two main things included in a PRM binder***
>
> ***describe five tips for writing clear PRM***

This unit has two sections:

- Flowcharting

- Programmer Ready Material (PRM)

A CBT unit will probably have the following elements:

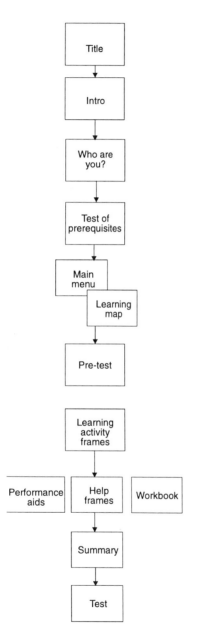

Use a representative graphic which embodies what the unit is about.

Outline the objectives and sell the benefits of the lesson, 'What it means to me', 'What I will be able to do'.

State the target group and provide separate routes for other users, e.g. managers, who want to browse through the material.

Test prerequisite knowledge, and don't let people continue until they pass.

Allow the learner to control his or her own learning from now on.

To see if the learner can master the objectives already.

Not teaching, but activities where the student can learn by discovery or doing in conjunction with a workbook and performance aids.

Reference information.

On-line help screens, possibly summarizing what is in the workbook.

Test to assess mastery of the objectives (the criterion test).

The diagram on the previous page is a simple flowchart

We draw flowcharts for CBT, interactive video and multimedia to check that:

- there are no loops
- all the responses are considered
- to let the programmer know where everything goes and how it links together

Start with an overview like the one on page 236, then produce more detailed flowcharts for the relevant elements.

Standard flowchart symbols

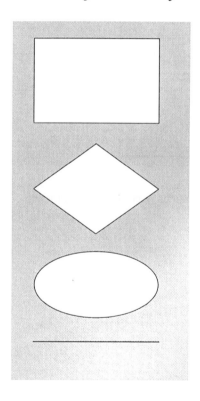

Represents information presented to the learner.

Represents routeing decisions or shows that a response is needed.

Represents the beginning or end of a lesson.

Represents the direction of student flow through the lesson.

Note: Flow lines never cross.

Branching

Use the flowcharts to show the branching involved in your unit, depending on the learner's response, e.g.:

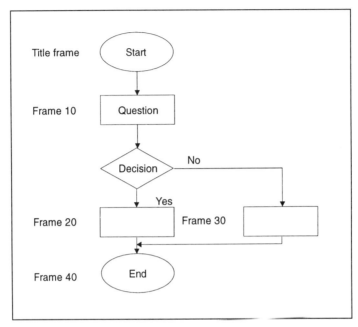

Label your frame numbers 10, 20, 30, etc. to allow room for additional frames, just like in programming.

How to draw a flowchart

- Make your flowchart fit on one page to make it easier to follow
- A box does not necessarily represent one screen
- If a sequence of screens is complex write a separate flowchart
- Put the following at the top left-hand corner of each page:
  - The page number. Your base flowchart should be No. 1
  - The coordinate for the left-hand axis of the matrix. This will always be a letter
  - The coordinate for the upper axis. This will always be a number

e.g.   1 B 1 refers to the symbol in B1 on page No. 1.

Flowchart

<table>
<tr><td>**Module name:**
Demonstration
First level flowchart Sheet 1</td><td>**Designer:**
Judith</td></tr>
</table>

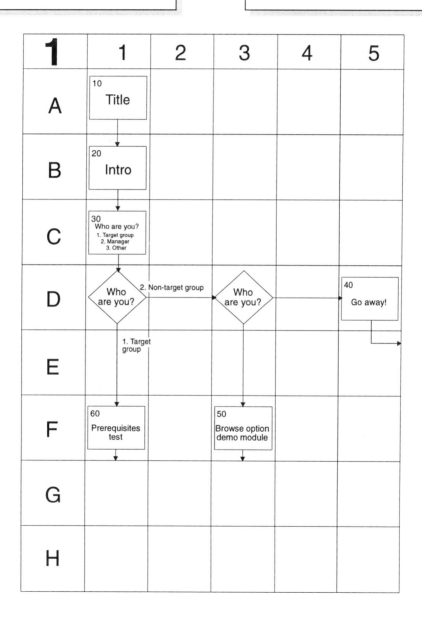

Flowchart

Module name:	Designer:
Demonstration	Judith
of 1 F 1	

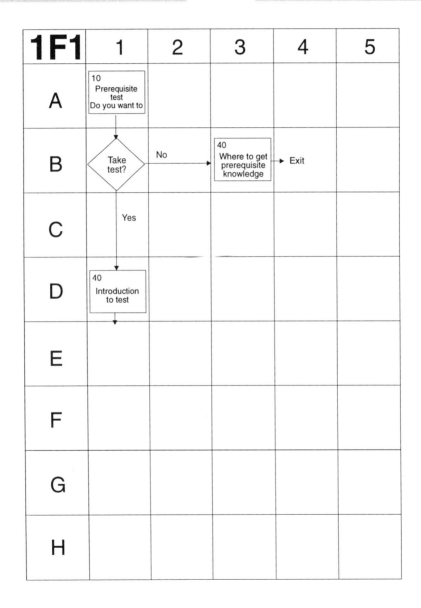

1F1	1	2	3	4	5
A	10 Prerequisite test Do you want to				
B	Take test? — No →		40 Where to get prerequisite knowledge → Exit		
C	Yes				
D	40 Introduction to test				
E					
F					
G					
H					

Don't be bound by convention

If traditional flowcharting does not work for you then use your own variation.

In practice I use combined flowchart/screen design outlines, e.g.:

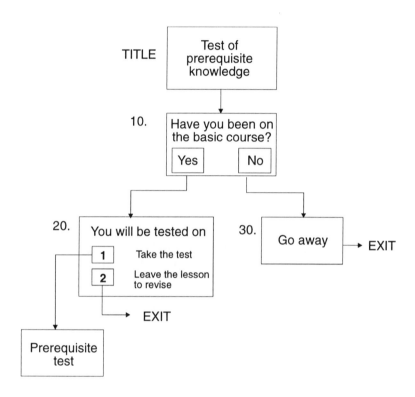

Draw a flowchart for any CBT part of your project.

Discuss it with a colleague. This is the main objective for this unit.

Programmer Ready Material (PRM)

Now that you can design a flowchart you will need to pass the complete lesson design to your developer/programmer. This is called Programmer Ready Material (PRM) and includes flowcharts and attached screen displays designed on screen design sheets.

An example of a simple CBT design sheet

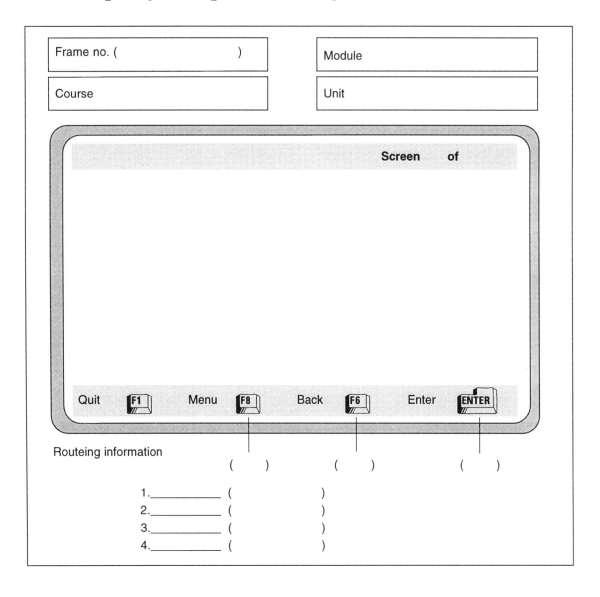

Example of a more sophisticated CBT design sheet used at Rediffusion Simulation

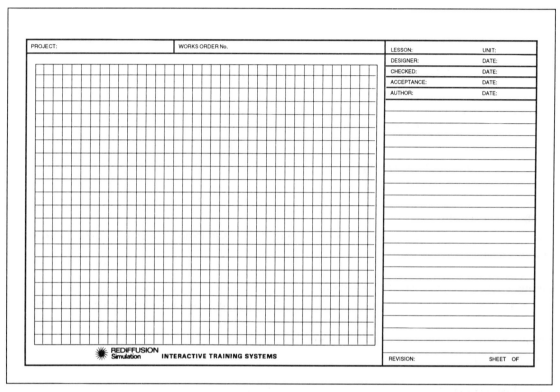

© *Rediffusion Simulation*

How much detail do you include in your PRM?

It depends on how confident you are in your programmer.

I prefer to give the basic information and leave issues such as colour, text size, layout, etc. to his or her creativity, as long as the principles of good screen design are followed.

Some hints and tips about writing PRM

Do not use coloured pens
The page may be photocopied!

Put the module name on every page
In case the pages get muddled up.

Number each screen
A good numbering system is 10, 20, 30, 40, etc. Later, if you need to add in a screen between 10 and 20 you can number it 15.

Eliminate text which has been crossed out
Your programmer may think that you want the student to see a crossed-out word! Use correction fluid.

Indicate where you want feedback to appear
In a consistent place.

State clearly which is the correct response to a question
It may not be obvious to the programmer.

Indicate how many times the learner can give a wrong response, e.g.:

He or she cannot move on until the correct answer is given.

If the learner answers wrong twice, give the right answer before moving on.

First time wrong	_____	feedback is 'no, try again'
Second time wrong	_____	feedback is a hint
Third time wrong	_____	feedback is the correct answer

To store the learner's response for later use
Indicate on the screen where you collect the response and state where it will be used.

For each test state the standard of mastery
You may want the learner to go back to the previous section if his or her performance is below a certain level.

Use your screen numbers to indicate the route(s) from each display, e.g.:

```
Screen 30

        Next          40
        Back          20
        Shift-back    10
        Help          35
```

If a screen is repeated
Give the frame number where it is to be used again.

Bind the PRM together with the flowchart
So that it cannot get mixed up.

Design for multimedia

You can design a multimedia lesson using very simple and accessible software, e.g. *Toolbook*.

The free word processor which comes with *Windows*, *Write © Microsoft*, allows you to drive graphics, sound and video.

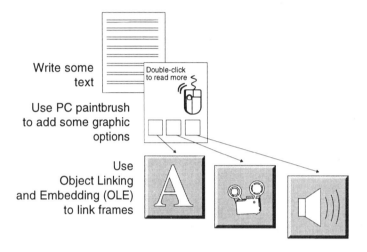

Write some text

Use PC paintbrush to add some graphic options

Use Object Linking and Embedding (OLE) to link frames

You will need a combined screen design/flowchart similar to CBT but with more options.

Structure

You need a mental picture of the structure of your program. This will probably look hierarchical when you draw it but it can still be totally flexible for the learner. Put this at the front of your flowcharts. Your challenge as a designer is to help learners keep a clear picture in their heads of the course structure, while still allowing them the freedom to roam around it, e.g.:

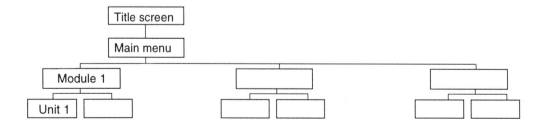

Beware multimedia teaching!

Voice instructions, high-quality photographs, hypertext that allows 'hot words' make multimedia a very seductive teaching machine. The danger is that it may be used in this way to teach or tell the student via the PC.

Multimedia is also very good at giving access to vast amounts of information, both in visual and text form. However, we have seen that good instructional design involves reducing the amount of knowledge a learner needs to a minimum. There is a danger that multimedia could encourage the sort of educational, knowledge-intensive training that Open Learning has been breaking down.

Multimedia is not the answer on its own

It is excellent for interactive access to vast amounts of information.

I wonder if training programmes with specific objectives could perhaps use multimedia reference banks to allow students to learn by discovery. For example, GCSE music classes may set students a quiz to find certain information. The students then use the *Musical Instruments* CD to find the relevant information for their course. We may find training programmes dipping into generic CDs as part of their courses.

Good learning materials should always involve a mix of media

Even with multimedia, learners will want workbooks to take away and hard-copy quick reference guides to use at short notice.

Multimedia is not the ultimate Open Learning delivery method but one of several options you should consider

Good design for multimedia is the same as for all other methods. The *CDI Designers Guide* (McGraw-Hill, 1993) says of instructional design: 'The term now carries connotations of CBT and Interactive Video which Multimedia designers eschew, but any of the fundamental principles of instructional design are relevant in any platform, whether the end product be a children's game, an electronic brochure or a training package.'

This book is about the fundamental instructional design you will need to make your multimedia objective. This is no different from any other method.

Quiz

1. Draw the standard flowchart symbols for the following:

    a.   Information

    b.   Decision

    c.   End of lesson

2. What does PRM stand for?

3. Give five tips for writing clear PRM.

    1.

    2.

    3.

    4.

    5.

Answers

---

1. Draw the standard flowchart symbols for the following

    a.   *Information*

    b.   *Decision*

    c.   *End of lesson*

2. What does PRM stand for?

    Programmer Ready Material

3. Give five tips for writing clear PRM

    1.   *Do not use coloured pens*
    2.   *Lesson name on every page*
    3.   *Number each frame*
    4.   *For complex displays, draw individual components, then the final screen*
    5.   *Use correction fluid, don't cross out unwanted text*
    6.   *Indicate where feedback should appear*
    7.   *State your short correct and incorrect feedback*
    8.   *State the correct response clearly*
    9.   *Indicate how many times the student can give a wrong response*
    10.   *Indicate where you want to collect responses*
    11.   *State conditions for mastery of tests*
    12.   *Put routing on each screen on the flowchart*
    13.   *Indicate repeated frames*
    14.   *Bind it!*

How to Design
Effective Open Learning

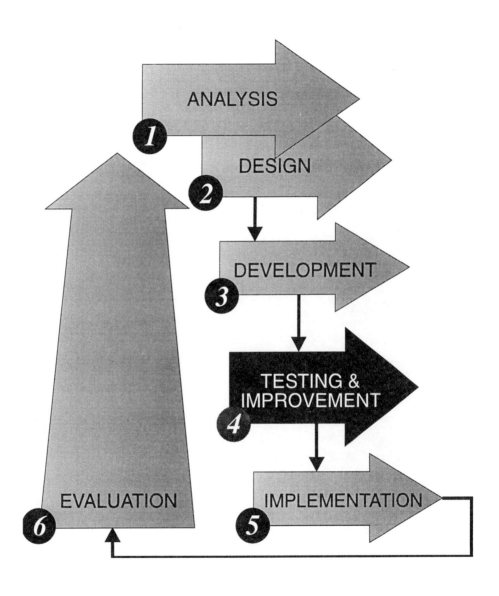

Module 4

Module 4 Testing and improvement

Do your training materials keep having to be changed? This unit will show you how to plan the testing and improvement phase so that this doesn't happen.

Objective

By the end of this module you will be able to:

describe the main steps in the testing and improvement phase

name two of the three other terms used to describe this stage

state who should sign off your draft materials before they are used for testing

Testing and improvement

The next step is to test and improve our learning material. Some people call this stage **validation, product evaluation** or **formative evaluation.**

Make sure you plan enough time for this phase

It is very important to plan enough time for this phase on the project plan. Once a manager or customer sees a lesson he or she is in danger of thinking that it is finished and may put pressure on you to release it and start another project. However, the testing phase is critical to good Open Learning. Unlike traditional training which can be easily modified at a later date, Open Learning has to stand on its own.

- Don't design for nine weeks and test for one week. If it takes five weeks to produce the first draft - allow five weeks for testing and editing!

- Don't be surprised if you end up taking 30 per cent of the total project time in testing and editing.

Design one module first and test with your high performer and SME and representatives from your target group to make sure that you are on the right lines. I would also show it to your customer or signatory. This could save a lot of time if it is not what they had in mind!

How to test and improve your material

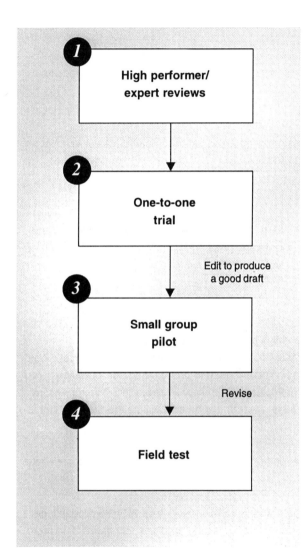

Check your rough design with your high performer.

Then check for technical accuracy with your SME.

Ask a member of the target group to try the draft material and make careful notes of what needs to be improved. You may do two or three of these.

A small group of learners use the material for real. You collect feedback.

Answer questions:

- Can the learner achieve the objectives?
- Does he or she like the product?
- Are the test questions reliable and valid?

The four stages in more detail

1. High performer/expert review

High performer

Check with your high performer that you have captured what he or she meant. Remember to keep things in his or her language. Write down what he or she says, not what you think you ought to write.

Subject matter expert (SME)

An expert cannot judge the effectiveness of your design; only the target group can do that. Ask him or her to check for technical accuracy, inaccuracies or omissions.

Editorial review

It is useful at this stage for the course designer or editor to go through the entire course to identify any problems of inconsistent format, unclear directions, missing material and poor style.

2. One-to-one trials

These are so called because you sit with a representative sample of the target group, one-to-one, while they go through the rough draft material. Look for any hesitation, misunderstanding or difficulty with the material. Watch the learners' faces. You will need to prompt them for feedback. 'You seemed to hesitate then, why?' Students are often reluctant to comment because they think they may expose their weaknesses. You must encourage a supportive atmosphere: 'It will be the material that is wrong, not you; we will change it.'

Ironic as it may sound, it can be good to have a pair of learners as they tend to talk to each other about the lesson and you can eavesdrop.

This is the first time you will get any idea of how long your lesson may take. You will also probably get far more comments and changes than you expected. Do not be discouraged - expect them. The more changes you make to suit your target group's needs, the more successful your lessons will be!

The more one-to-one tests you can do, the better. You also need to make sure that your tests are suitable for representatives of your target group. It is no use testing your material with your graduate-level colleagues in the office if the target group is GCSE-level clerks!

3.   Small group pilots

These look for major problems such as omissions, inappropriate examples, inconsistencies, poor questions and passive writing. They also validate how well students can meet the objectives. Ideally you should try to test the material on about ten members of the target group.

4.   Field testing

This involves large numbers of learners from the target population being tested under the actual conditions. It allows you to validate that the material really is effective for the students for whom it was designed.

Use questionnaires to collect feedback.

Collect all your comments, make further revisions and compose the final package.

Last check

Now test the final package again and make sure you get this signed off by:

- the Subject Matter Expert

- the customer

before you release it to the target group for full implementation.

Implementation

Even at this stage you should include feedback sheets so that students can send you their comments and suggestions. This is another phase of validation.

There is a simple example on page 258.

Example of a validation sheet

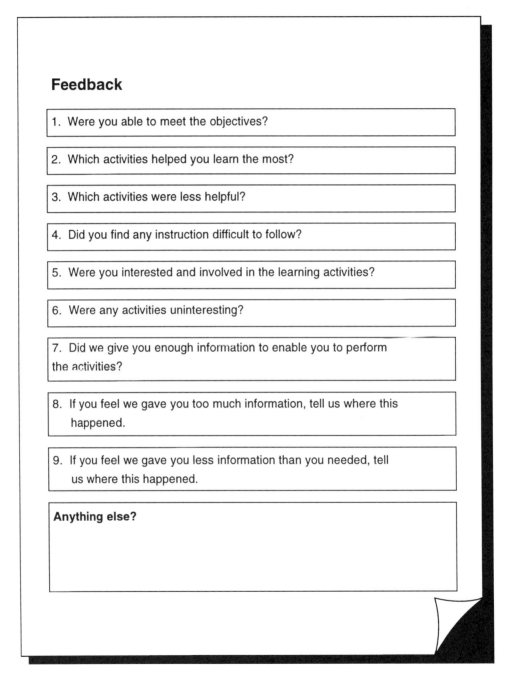

Feedback

1. Were you able to meet the objectives?

2. Which activities helped you learn the most?

3. Which activities were less helpful?

4. Did you find any instruction difficult to follow?

5. Were you interested and involved in the learning activities?

6. Were any activities uninteresting?

7. Did we give you enough information to enable you to perform the activities?

8. If you feel we gave you too much information, tell us where this happened.

9. If you feel we gave you less information than you needed, tell us where this happened.

Anything else?

Quiz

1. **Describe the main steps in the testing and improvement phase.**

2. **Name two other terms used to describe the testing and improvement stage.**

3. **Who should sign off your draft materials before they are used for testing?**

4. **When does validation take place?**

Answers

1. Describe the main steps in the testing and improvement phase.

> 1. High performer/expert reviews
> 2. One-to-one trials
> 3. Small group pilots
> 4. Field testing

2. Name two other terms used to describe the testing and improvement stage.

> • Formative evaluation
> • Validation
> • Product evaluation

3. Who should sign off your draft materials before they are used for testing?

> Subject matter expert
> High performer

4. When does validation take place?

> All through this phase, but particularly in small group pilots,
> field testing and implementation

How to Design
Effective Open Learning

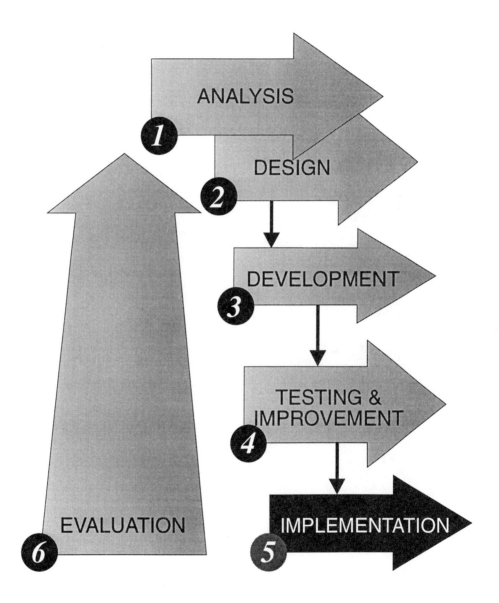

Module 5

Module 5 Implementation

- **Unit 1**

Implementation support

- **Unit 2**

Project management

Unit 1

Implementation support

Have you ever wondered what happened to your training, whether you should have provided more support to aid its success? Read on ...

Objective

By the end of this unit you will be able to:

describe the training designer's involvement in implementation

state when you find out about environmental factors which might hinder implementation

What is the designer's involvement in implementation?

Traditionally the customer is responsible for the successful implementation of the solutions.

However, the designer should not 'opt out' completely. He or she has a valuable role to play:

1.   In the small group pilots and field tests

To collect data about other things that are needed to ensure successful implementation, e.g. to design supporting materials for people outside the target group but who form part of the target audience, such as managers' guides, customer leaflets, trainers' notes, etc.

2.   During the launch

To support the management team, possibly by explaining how the learning materials will be used.

3.   During implementation

Arrange regular reviews (say, once every four to six weeks) with your customer and users to see how the solution is going. Collect evidence of success, because successful solutions often become invisible and are not thought of as training, just 'It's the way we do things around here.'

4.   In evaluation

To make sure that the evaluation meeting you set up in the analysis phase actually takes place.

If the solutions are not proving effective, you might have to remind your customer about some of the environmental factors that you identified in the analysis. Has the incentive structure been changed? Does completion of the learning modules appear on people's performance reviews?

Quiz

---

1. **What is the training designer's involvement in implementation? Fill in the blanks.**

   Traditionally the customer is responsible for implementation, but the training designer should:

   •

   •

   •   **support the launch**

   •

   •   **design additional materials or interventions if necessary**

Answers

1. *What is the training designer's involvement in implementation? Fill in the blanks.*

> *Traditionally the customer is responsible for implementation, but the training designer should:*
>
> •   *collect data in the small group pilots and field tests about things that might hinder implementation*
>
> •   *design supporting materials for other members of the target audience, e.g. instructors' notes or managers' guides*
>
> •   *support the launch*
>
> •   *design additional materials or interventions if necessary*

Unit 2

Project management

Objective

By the end of this unit you will be able to:

*- describe a simple method for ensuring that every module follows
the correct design process*

- describe all the roles on a design project plan

*- list five of the first nine steps on the design checklist
for text-based material*

A project team

The stages in a systematic approach provide a very good framework to manage Open Learning projects.

First, they allow you to identify the different roles involved and to set up a team with the required skills. A normal split for a project team will be:

- project manager/analyst

- designers

- developers (programmers, desktop publishers, video specialists)

Some hints on managing projects

We will not go into project management in detail here. The skills are the same for managing any project, and if you are going to manage an Open Learning design project you should consider getting some generic project-management training.

Some important hints:

- Do not underestimate the time needed for testing and editing. Allow 30-50 per cent of the project time for this.

- Try and plan for slippage in the project plan and have contingency plans ready:
  there is always slippage.

- Keep a frequent check on the progress against the project plan and if things are
  slipping take immediate action, e.g. sanction more overtime or extra resources.

There are many more, but that's the topic of another book.

A performance aid to help you manage projects

Below we have included an example of a performance aid that you might use to control your projects. We suggest you develop your own as well as page-design standards.

While you are at it, why not design a skeleton lesson showing your house style: for screen layout, use of colour, etc.?

Design checklist

Package: _____ Designer: _____

High performer: _____

Module: _____ SME: _____

Stage	Name	Signature	Date
Raw material from HP Rough design complete Word-processed version Designer check High performer check SME check One-to-one test One-to-one test Design edits			
DTP Version 1			
Designer check SME check Proof-reading Project manager check			
DTP Version 2			
Proof-reading Small group trials Design edits			
Final DTP Version			
Gold seal Customer - Signature			
DTP Prep for printing			
Printing Distribution			

How to put together a project plan

1. List your **activities**

e.g.	a.	Research with an SME
	b.	Rough design
	c.	Typing
	d.	SME check
	e.	One-to-one trial

2. List your **tasks**

e.g.	1.	Introduction
	2.	Module 1
	3.	Module 2
	4.	Module 3
	5.	Managers' guide
	6.	Workshop

3. List your **resources**

e.g.	Designer	-	Bobby
	SME	-	Christine
	Customer	-	Brenda
	Typist	-	Dee

4. Find some **project planning sheets** with enough space for one entry per day, e.g.:

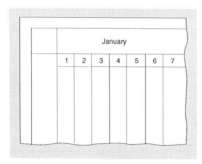

Example of a project plan

On page 275 is a real example of a project plan using software called *On Target © Symantec.*

Practical Instructional Design for Open Learning

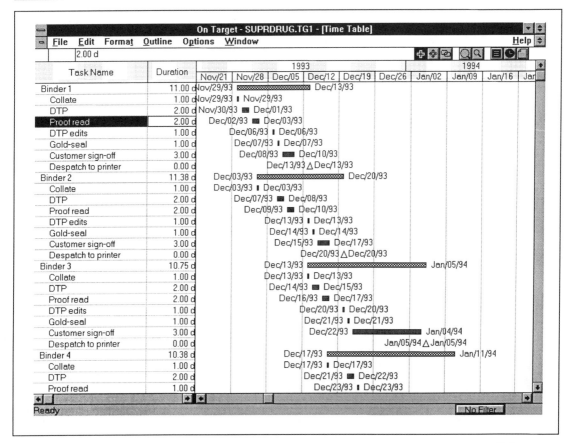

Quiz

1. **What simple method will ensure that every module follows the correct design process?**

2. *Describe all the roles on a design project plan.*

3. *Describe five of the nine steps on the design checklist that take place before desktop publishing (for text-based material).*

    -
    -
    -
    -
    -

Answers

1. **What simple method will ensure that every module follows the correct design process?**

   > *Add a design checklist to the front of each module and make sure each step is signed off.*

2. **Describe all the roles on a design project plan.**

   > *- Designer*
   > *- High performer*
   > *- Subject matter expert*
   > *- Sign-off*
   > *- Project manager*

3. **Describe five of the nine steps on the design checklist that take place before desktop publishing (for text-based material).**

   > •   *Raw material from high performer*
   > •   *Rough design complete*
   > •   *Word-processed version*
   > •   *Designer check*
   > •   *High performer check*
   > •   *SME check*
   > •   *One-to-one trial*
   > •   *One-to-one trial*
   > •   *Design edits*
   >
   >
   > *See design checklist on page 273.*

How to Design
Effective Open Learning

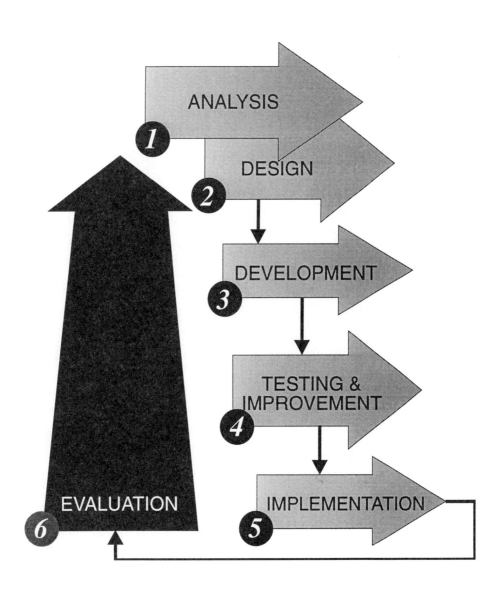

M o d u l e   6

Module 6 Evaluation

Have you ever thought evaluation of training was difficult? This unit will explode that myth and show you how to do it.

Objective

By the end of this module you will be able to:

describe the difference between validation and evaluation

state when the key activities in evaluation take place

name those with whom you hold summative evaluation meetings

describe when you set up data collection for evaluation

describe why trainers often find evaluation difficult

describe what you evaluate in evaluation

What is the difference between validation and evaluation?

Validation
Checking that the form of the learner's materials is valid, that they help the learner to achieve the objectives.

Evaluation
Has the desired performance been achieved? This is sometimes called *summative evaluation.*

When does validation take place?

See Module 4 because most validation takes place in:

- small group pilots
- field testing
- implementation

plus interviews after implementation.

Two ways to do this are:

1. A test/quiz
2. A feedback sheet

Try the final quiz and feedback sheet for this book.

We are now going to validate this book.

Try the following quiz on the content. You will also find a feedback sheet on page 309.

Summative evaluation

The technical name for evaluation is summative evaluation because we look at the **summed** effects of the solutions within an organization.

Your learning package will contribute to improving someone's performance.

Evaluation begins in the analysis phase! You can only evaluate whether the target group has achieved the desired performance if this was defined in the analysis style.

The key activities in analysis are to define the measurable criterion by which you will know that the desired performance has been achieved. Think back to our DPI example. The desired performance was:

All sales people can sell this product because they all pass the test and are licensed. Company sales targets of £3.5 million achieved and annual sales targets for all regions achieved for DPI.

Who do we hold evaluation meetings with?

Whoever can answer the question 'Has the desired performance been achieved?'

In our example it would probably be the sales director. It should always be your customer.

What about setting up data collection for evaluation?

This needs to be done in the analysis phase. For example, if no one knows how many salespeople are licensed to sell DPI how can we tell whether we have been successful?

Why do trainers find evaluation difficult?

1. Because they do not do a thorough enough analysis and have not set up the criterion by which to measure that the desired performance has been achieved.

2. Because they try to evaluate training, which is nonsense because what we need to evaluate is performance or the **effect** of training on helping to improve performance.

Training is only one factor in helping to improve performance.

You cannot evaluate training, it is only a 'how to', not an end result.

Quiz

1. **Describe the difference between validation and evaluation.**

   Validation:

   Evaluation:

2. **State when the key activities in evaluation take place.**

3. **Name those with whom you hold summative evaluation meetings.**

4. **When do you set up data collection for evaluation?**

5. **Why do trainers often find evaluation difficult?**

6. **What do you evaluate in evaluation?**

Answers

1. **Describe the difference between validation and evaluation.**

   > Validation: Checking that the form of the learning materials
   >   is valid, that they help the learner to achieve the
   >   objectives
   >
   > Evaluation: Has the desired performance been achieved?
   >   It is sometimes called summative evaluation

2. **State when the key activities in evaluation take place.**

   > In the analysis phase

3. **Name those with whom you hold summative evaluation meetings.**

   > Your customer

4. **When do you set up data collection for evaluation?**

   > In the analysis phase

5. **Why do trainers often find evaluation difficult?**

   > Because they often do not define the desired performance in
   > the analysis phase

6. **What do you evaluate in evaluation?**

   > Performance, not training

Summary

This book cannot cover the skill of designing effective text-based Open Learning. It can only provide essential knowledge and some performance aids. However, these are useless until they are used, and to develop skilled performance you need practice and feedback.

So you really need to work on our projects, use the book as a performance aid, and preferably get some personal coaching from a skilled designer.

Try and find someone in your organization to help. Or find out details of ACT's workshops and consultancy.

Producing an effective Open Learning lesson involves many skills. It's a bit like watching the credits at the end of a film. Many people have been involved in a successful product.

Don't try and do it all yourself, you will fail!

Your team will take time to perfect the skills involved, but following the systematic approach in this book will help you avoid the major pitfalls and produce effective lessons.

On the next page is a summary of all the stages involved.

A summary of the stages

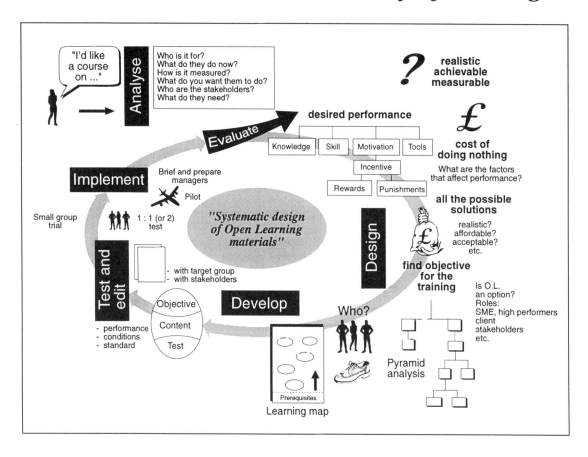

Summary

A systematic approach to designing training material

1.   Analysis

- Describe the problem
- Define the problem in performance terms
- Write a measurable final objective
- Describe the target group

2.   Design

- Check for other existing or possible solutions
- Use pyramid analysis to break down the objective into topics
- Write subordinate objectives
- Group sub-objectives according to learning type
- Choose media for each module
- Check the potential for using performance aids
- Write tests for each module, *then* the learning objectives

3.   Development

- Produce the materials for each module

4.   Testing and improvement

- One-to-one trials and small group pilots
- Revise

5.   Implementation

- Implement

6.   Evaluation

- Evaluate after a suitable period of use to see whether the desired performance has been achieved

Final quiz

Test your knowledge. Refer back to the modules if you need any help.

1. Label the stages in the systematic approach to training design.

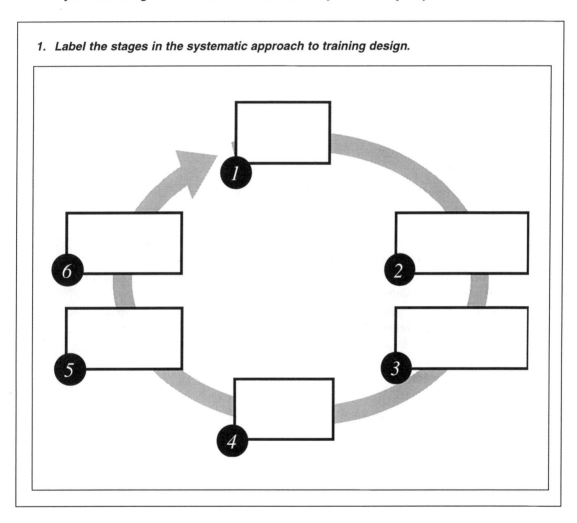

Final quiz

2. **Match each phrase with the appropriate definition below.**

1. *Analysis*

2. *Design*

3. *Development*

4. *Testing and improvement*

5. *Implementation*

6. *Summative evaluation*

a. *A detailed plan of the course is produced, including the choice of media.*
b. *The course is used by the target audience in the intended environment.*
c. *The effectiveness of the course in solving the performance problem is measured.*
d. *Draft forms of the training material are prepared for the student trials.*
e. *The final objective is agreed and other solutions to the problem outlined.*
f. *Small groups of the target audience check the material for completeness and accuracy.*

3. **What is the performance gap?**

The difference between

the

and

Final quiz

4. *Describe one of the first three causes of low performance.*

5. *Name three of the key factors that might justify using Open Learning.*

1.

2.

3.

6. *What is an SME?*

7. *What is a high performer?*

Final quiz

8.   What is the difference between the target population and the target group?

The target population is:

The target group is:

9.   State four elements of measurable objective.

    1.

    2.

    3.

    4.

10.   What question do you repeatedly ask yourself when analysing a pyramid of topics?

11.   What are the two fundamentally different types of learning which affect how you design learning materials?

Final quiz

12. Complete the following list of essential steps for effective instruction:

    1.   **Sell the benefits**

    2.   **Check the** [   ]

    3.   **Introduce - state the** [   ] **objective**

    4.   **Present learning activities for the new skills or knowledge**

    5.   **Demonstrate or model the** [   ] **performance and test understanding**

    6.   **Provide** [   ] **and feedback**

    7.   [   ] **that the performance objective can be mastered**

13. What are the following examples of?

    •   *a checklist*

    •   *a printed form*

    •   *a label*

14. When designing a module, after writing the objectives what do you do next?

Final quiz

15.   **What is the most important factor in selecting media?**

16.   **What is the most critical thing about question design?**

17.   **Rewrite the following in the active voice, personal style.**

It is important that all text appearing on the page is written with the rules for conciseness clearly in mind.

Final quiz

18.   **What are the four stages of testing and improvement?**

1.

2.

3.

4.

This is the end!

How did you do?

Answers

Test your knowledge. Refer back to the modules if you need any help.

1. Label the stages in the systematic approach to training design.

```
                    ┌──────────────┐
                    │   ANALYSIS   │
                    └──────────────┘
                         ①
        ┌──────────────┐              ┌──────────────┐
        │  EVALUATION  │              │    DESIGN    │
        └──────────────┘              └──────────────┘
             ⑥                             ②

     ┌──────────────────┐          ┌──────────────┐
     │  IMPLEMENTATION  │          │ DEVELOPMENT  │
     └──────────────────┘          └──────────────┘
             ⑤                             ③
                    ┌──────────────┐
                    │  TESTING &   │
                    │ IMPROVEMENT  │
                    └──────────────┘
                         ④
```

Answers

2. Match each phrase with the appropriate definition below.

1. **Analysis** | e |

2. **Design** | a |

3. **Development** | d |

4. **Testing and improvement** | f |

5. **Implementation** | b |

6. **Summative evaluation** | c |

a. A detailed plan of the course is produced, including the choice of media.
b. The course is used by the target audience in the intended environment.
c. The effectiveness of the course in solving the performance problem is measured.
d. Draft forms of the training material are prepared for the student trials.
e. The final objective is agreed and other solutions to the problem outlined.
f. Small groups of the target audience check the material for completeness and accuracy.

3. What is the performance gap?

The difference between

| the | desired performance |

| and | actual performance |

Answers

4. Describe one of the first three causes of low performance.

1. Poor information/unclear expectations
2. Difficult environment/inadequate equipment
3. Poor incentives
4. Lack of knowledge
5. Lack of skills
6. Poor motivation

5. Name three of the key factors that might justify using Open Learning.

1. A large target group

2. Geographically dispersed

3. The training needs to be repeated often

4. The material has a long shelf-life

5. People want to enter training with variable levels of skill and knowledge

6. People need to learn at their own pace, place and time

6. What is an SME?

Subject matter expert

7. What is a high performer?

Somebody who already does the job well

Answers

8. **What is the difference between the target population and the target group?**

   The target population is:

   > All the people who may use the course

   The target group is:

   > The main users of the course

9. **State four elements of measurable objective.**

   > 1. Conditions
   >
   > 2. Performance
   >
   > 3. Standard
   >
   > 4. Method of assessment

10. **What question do you repeatedly ask yourself when analysing a pyramid of topics?**

    > What does the person need to be able to do in order to perform at this higher level?

11. **What are the two fundamentally different types of learning which affect how you design learning materials?**

    > • Knowledge
    >
    > • Skills

Answers

12. **Complete the following list of essential steps for effective instruction:**

    1. **Sell the benefits**

    2. **Check the** | **prerequisites** |

    3. **Introduce - state the** | **performance** | **objective**

    4. **Present learning activities for the new skills or knowledge**

    5. **Demonstrate or model the** | **desired** | **performance and test understanding**

    6. **Provide** | **practice** | **and feedback**

    7. | **Test** | **that the performance objective can be mastered**

13. **What are the following examples of?**

    - **a checklist**

    - **a printed form**   **Performance aids**

    - **a label**

14. **When designing a module, after writing the objectives, what do you do next?**

    Design the test

Answers

15. *What is the most important factor in selecting media?*

> That it is as close to the real performance as possible.

16. *What is the most critical thing about question design?*

> That questions come directly from the performance objective and are relevant tests of the desired performance

17. *Rewrite the following in the active voice, personal style.*

It is important that all text appearing on the page is written with the rules for conciseness clearly in mind.

> Write it concisely

Answers

18.   What are the four stages of testing and improvement?

1.   Expert/high performer review

2.   One-to-one trials

3.   Small group trials

4.   Piloting

Bibliography

This book is a collection of applied theory from numerous sources over the years. I have been influenced by many designers and helped by suggestions from countless students on my workshops.

Anderson Seiler, B. *Guidelines for Designing PLATO Lessons.* University of Delaware, 1981.

Avner, R.A. 'How to produce ineffective CAL material', *Educational Technology*, August 1971.

Beech, G. *Computer Based Learning.* Sigma Technical Press, 1983.

Boydell, T.H. *A Guide to Job Analysis*. Bacie, 1973.

Boydell, T.H. *A Guide to the Identification of Training Needs*. Bacie, 1973.

Carter, R. *Systems Management and Change*, P.C.P. Paul Chapman Ltd. in association with The Open University

Control Data Corporation Courseware Development Process, 1979.

Dean, C. and Whitlock, Q. *A Handbook of Computer Based Training*, 2nd edition. Kogan Page, 1988.

Fletcher, Shirley, *Designing Competence Based Training*, Kogan Page, 1991.

Heines, J. 'Writing objectives with style', *Training*, December 1979.

Heines, J.M. *Screen Design Strategies for Computer Assisted Instruction.* Digital Press, 1984.

Heines, J. 'Anybody can't do CBT. A team approach to course development', *Training News*, March 1985.

Heines, J. 'Interactive means active, learner involvement in CBT data', *Training*, March 1985.

Hottos, S. *CD-I Designers Guide.* McGraw-Hill, 1993.

Mager, R.F. *Preparing Instructional Objectives.* David S. Lake Publishers, 1984.

Mager, R.F. and Beech, G. *Developing Vocational Instruction*, 1st edition, Fearon Publishers, 1967.

Mager, R.F. and Pipe, P. *Analysing Performance Problems.* David S. Lake Publishers, 1970.

Mager, R.F. and Pipe, P. *Performance Analysis Flowchart*. David S. Lake Publishers, 1979.

Mager, R.F. and Pipe, P. *Performance Analysis Worksheet.* David S. Lake Publishers, 1979.

Romiszowski, A. J. *Designing Instructional Systems.* Kogan Page, 1981.

Romiszowski, A. J. *Developing Auto-Instructional Materials.* Kogan Page, 1986.

THE END

Credits

With thanks to Paul for his brilliant page layout and desktop publishing.

To Judith, Tom, Elsie and Charles for putting up with me while I was working on the book.

Feedback sheet

Your feedback is very important to us. Please could you spare some time to answer the following questions:

1. **What is your overall impression of the book? Is it of value to you?**

2. **What contributed most to your learning?**

3. **What contributed least?**

4. **What do you suggest we improve and how?**

Summary

Any other comments?

Name and address

Thank you for your help.

Please return to:

Nigel Harrison
32 Victoria Road
Broomhall
Sheffield
S10 2DL

Further titles in the McGraw-Hill Training Series

THE BUSINESS OF TRAINING
Achieving Success in Changing World Markets
Trevor Bentley   ISBN 0-07-707328-2

EVALUATING TRAINING EFFECTIVENESS
Translating Theory into Practice
Peter Bramley   ISBN 0-07-707331-2

DEVELOPING EFFECTIVE TRAINING SKILLS
Tony Pont   ISBN 0-07-707383-5

MAKING MANAGEMENT DEVELOPMENT WORK
Achieving Success in the Nineties
Charles Margerison   ISBN 0-07-707382-7

MANAGING PERSONAL LEARNING AND CHANGE
A Trainer's Guide
Neil Clark   ISBN 0-07-707344-4

HOW TO DESIGN EFFECTIVE TEXT-BASED
OPEN LEARNING
A Modular Course
Nigel Harrison   ISBN 0-07-707355-X

HOW TO DESIGN EFFECTIVE COMPUTER-BASED
TRAINING:
A Modular Course
Nigel Harrison   ISBN 0-07-707354-1

HOW TO SUCCEED IN EMPLOYEE DEVELOPMENT
Moving from Vision to Results
Ed Moorby   ISBN 0-07-707459-9

USING VIDEO IN TRAINING AND EDUCATION
Ashly Pinnington   ISBN 0-07-707384-3

TRANSACTIONAL ANALYSIS FOR TRAINERS
Julie Hay   ISBN 0-07-707470-X

SELF-DEVELOPMENT
A Facilitator's Guide
Mike Pedler and
David Megginson   ISBN 0-07-707460-2

DEVELOPING WOMEN THROUGH TRAINING
A Practical Handbook
Liz Willis and
Jenny Daisley   ISBN 0-07-707566-8

DESIGNING AND ACHIEVING COMPETENCY
A Competency-Based Approach to Developing People and
Organizations
Editors: Rosemary Boam
and Paul Sparrow   ISBN 0-07-707572-2

TOTAL QUALITY TRAINING
The Quality Culture and Quality Trainer
Brian Thomas   ISBN 0-07-707472-6

CAREER DEVELOPMENT AND PLANNING
A Guide for Managers, Trainers and Personnel Staff
Malcolm Peel   ISBN 0-07-707554-4

SALES TRAINING
A Guide to Developing Effective Salespeople
Frank S. Salisbury   ISBN 0-07-707458-0

CLIENT-CENTRED CONSULTING
A Practical Guide for Internal Advisers and Trainers
Peter Cockman, Bill Evans
and Peter Reynolds   ISBN 0-07-707685-0

TRAINING TO MEET THE TECHNOLOGY CHALLENGE
Trevor Bentley   ISBN 0-07-707589-7

IMAGINATIVE EVENTS Volumes I & II
Ken Jones
                ISBN 0-07-707679-6 Volume I
                ISBN 0-07-707680-X Volume II
                ISBN 0-07-707681-8 for set of Volume I & II